Ephesians, Colossians, 2 Thessalonians, The Pastoral Epistles

PROCLAMATION COMMENTARIES

The New Testament Witnesses for Preaching   Gerhard Krodel, *Editor*

EPHESIANS, COLOSSIANS, 2 THESSALONIANS, THE PASTORAL EPISTLES

J. Paul Sampley

Joseph Burgess

Gerhard Krodel

Reginald H. Fuller

FORTRESS PRESS   Philadelphia, Pennsylvania

Library of Congress Cataloging in Publication Data

Main entry under title:
Ephesians, Colossians, 2 Thessalonians, the Pastoral
  epistles.
   (Proclamation commentaries)
   Bibliography: p.
   1. Bible. N.T. Ephesians—Criticism, interpretation,
etc.—Addresses, essays, lectures.   2. Bible. N.T.
Colossians—Criticism, interpretation, etc.—Addresses,
essays, lectures.   3. Bible. N.T. 2 Thessalonians—
Criticism, interpretation, etc.—Addresses, essays,
lectures.   4. Bible. N.T. Pastoral epistles—
Criticism, interpretation, etc.—Addresses, essays,
lectures.   I. Sampley, J. Paul.
BS2650.2.E63   227'.5'06   77-78652
ISBN 0-8006-0589-6

6446K77   Printed in the United States of America   1-589

CONTENTS

EDITOR'S FOREWORD

The letters discussed in this book bear Paul's name though there is widespread agreement that they were written by someone else under his name. Thus they give evidence of Paul's importance and influence in the generation which followed him. Each of the letters has shifted Paul's theological emphases into new directions and all are conscious of the authority of the apostolic tradition. This need for authoritative tradition in new situations was one of the factors which prompted the rise of pseudonymous letters.

The reader who would like to pursue the phenomenon of pseudonymity in early Christian literature may turn to articles such as: K. Aland in: *The Authorship and Integrity of the NT. Theol. Collections* 4 (London: SPCK, 1965) 1–13; B. M. Metzger in: *JBL* 91, 1972, 3 ff.; K. M. Fischer in: *NTS* 23, 1976, 76–81; N. Brox, *Pseudepigraphie in der heidnischen und juedisch-christlichen Antike.* (Darmstadt: Wissensch. Buchg. 1977).

The interpreters of these writings belong to different denominations even as the writings themselves exhibit diverse traditions. J. Paul Sampley, a Methodist, teaches at Indiana University. Joseph Burgess is a member of the faculty of the Lutheran Theological Seminary at Gettysburg, Pa. Reginald Fuller is professor of New Testament at the Protestant Episcopal Seminary in Virginia.

GERHARD KRODEL
Lutheran Theological Seminary,
Gettysburg, Pennsylvania

J. PAUL SAMPLEY

THE LETTER TO
THE EPHESIANS

INTRODUCTION

The document entitled "The Letter of Paul to the Ephesians" is
an enigma on several counts. First, according to the best Greek
manuscripts the actual text of the letter does not identify any
specific destination. We know the document by its superscrip-
tion—"The Letter of Paul to the Ephesians"—but the superscrip-
tions of the NT documents were added late in the second century.
In the best Greek manuscripts the text of the letter does not mention Ephesus. It simply opens: "Paul . . . to the saints who are
also faithful in Christ Jesus" (1:1). We do not know the identity
of the intended recipients. One of the earliest interpreters of
Paul, the second century heretic Marcion, thought this letter might
be the otherwise lost "letter to the Laodiceans" mentioned in
Col. 4:16. Although we do not know to whom the letter was
written, for convenience we will take the name Ephesians to refer
both to the document and to the recipients.

Not only do we not know who were the intended recipients of
the letter, we also cannot be sure exactly why it was written.
Paul's letters usually respond to a discernible and very specific
historical situation. A crisis or problem brought most Pauline
letters into existence. Even Romans, written to a church that
Paul's preaching did not establish, is a "bread-and-butter" letter
written in advance of his journey, seeking support for his mission
to Spain (cf. 15:22–24). Ephesians, however, lacks clues concerning a concrete crisis or occasion. There are urgings for unity
scattered through the letter (cf. esp. 4:1–16); perhaps there was
some threat to unity. But if there were such a threat, the clues
are so general that we cannot reconstruct the specifics. In 2:11 ff.
there is the assertion that Jews and gentiles are brought together

9

in Christ; was there fear of a Jewish-gentile split among the Christians for whom this letter was intended?   Again, we lack the information to tell whether this was the case or not.   In sum, therefore, the letter to the Ephesians is of a very general character. The precise historical purposes of its author are hidden from the modern reader.   Nevertheless, Ephesians became a widely quoted and appreciated letter among the early church fathers and has remained so down through history.

Although we have no answers to the questions to whom this letter was written and for what purpose it was drafted, the question of authorship seems less problematic at first glance.   The letter directly identifies Paul as the author: "Paul, an apostle of Christ Jesus by the will of God" (1:1).   And until Erasmus, the great sixteenth century scholar, that assignation was unquestioned: it was Paul who wrote Ephesians.   Erasmus noted such stylistic differences, however, that he concluded Ephesians was written by someone besides the Paul of the other letters.   From the seventeenth century to the present, the question has been debated.   As the situation now stands, scholars are divided—and no doubt will continue to be because the issue is not decisively demonstrable one way or the other.   Whatever one's decision on the authorship of Ephesians, it must be made in comparison with the undoubtedly authentic Pauline letters—Romans, 1 and 2 Corinthians, Galatians, Philippians, 1 Thessalonians, and Philemon—and in conjunction with Colossians, the letter to which it has greatest affinities.

Since the letter declares itself Pauline, the burden of proof lies with those who would question its explicit claim.   The problems with Pauline attribution of Ephesians focus around the following issues: 1) peculiar style and vocabulary; and 2) distinctive assertions.

Peculiar Style and Vocabulary

The student of the Greek text is immediately struck by the complex and long sentences that make up Ephesians.   While common in Ephesians, such constructions are relatively infrequent in the unquestioned Pauline letters.   Like delicate and complicated filigrees, the sentences are composed of appositional phrases, genitival constructions, and relative clauses interwoven with one another and hanging from one or two central verbs. Eph. 1:15–23 is an example of one such sentence. In this sentence the RSV translators have preserved the sentence intact, though that is not always their pattern (cf. 4:11-16).

The vocabulary of Ephesians at times seems strange on two counts. First, Ephesians contains a fair number of words that, though they are entirely missing from the undisputed Pauline letters, are found frequently in the later writings of the NT and in the early church fathers. These words seem to represent a half-way house between the unquestioned Pauline letters and the second century church. They include such terms as "commonwealth" (*politeia*, 2:11; cf. *politeuma* in Phil. 3:20), "likeness" (*hosiotes*, 4:24), "debauchery" (*asōtia*, 5:18), and "be tossed here and there by waves" (*kludōnizomai*, 4:14).

But the vocabulary of Ephesians is strange on another count as well. The author of Ephesians may employ a different term or phrase in place of the one that would be expected from the unquestioned Pauline correspondence, or he may introduce terms not present in the other letters. One very noticeable example is his tendency to use "heavenly places" (*ta epouraniois*, 1:3, 20; 2:6; 3:10; and 6:12) where Paul generally refers to "heaven" (*ouranos*; cf., for example, Rom. 1:18, Gal. 1:8 and Phil. 3:20; but contrast 1 Cor. 15:40, 48, 49). For introduction of terms not present in the other letters, consider the designation of Christ as "the Beloved" (1:6, *ho ēgapēmenos*) or the use of the Semitic "flesh and blood" (6:12) as a euphemism for "people."

Distinctive Assertions

Style and vocabulary aside, more weighty objections to the Pauline authorship of Ephesians center on some of the assertions made in that letter. Perhaps most striking in this regard is the disappearance of the expected imminent end of the world that marks the indisputably authentic Pauline letters (cf. 1 Thess. 4:13 ff., 1 Cor. 7:26, 29, 31; 15:51–52 and 2 Cor. 4:17). Although the culmination of God's purposes is of interest to Ephesians (cf. 1:10), the imminent end of history is not the author's way of conveying that concern. Linked directly to Ephesians' depreciation of the heavy Pauline emphasis on the impending end of history is Ephesians' insistence that the believers *already* share not only Christ's death (so the unquestionably authentic Pauline letters) but also his resurrection (unlike those Pauline letters). More on this below, but here note Eph. 2:5-6 "God made us alive together with Christ (by grace you have been saved), and raised us up with him, and made us sit with him in the heavenly places in Christ Jesus."

Some interpreters find other claims in Ephesians difficult to reconcile with the indisputably authentic Pauline letters. For example, the lofty view of marriage set forward in Eph. 5:22-33 jars one's mind when seen alongside 1 Corinthians 1. In the latter, Paul condones marriage as an outlet for passions that are otherwise uncontrollable, but says it would be better if one could simply give undivided attention to "the Lord" and remain unmarried (1 Cor. 7:8-9, 32-38). In a similar way, Ephesians' near veneration of the apostles is somewhat out of joint with Paul's view of apostleship in general and his own in particular. In Ephesians they are dubbed "holy apostles" (3:5) and, along with the prophets, are said to be the foundation of the church while Christ is called the cornerstone (2:20; contrast 1 Cor. 3:11).

These are some of the problems that interpreters have found with assigning the letter to the Ephesians to Pauline authorship. Though the case for or against Pauline authorship of Ephesians will fall short of proof, the problems seem to outweigh the similarities. Accordingly, we will proceed on the assumption that although Paul probably did not write Ephesians, it was very likely composed by a close follower of his who, in Paul's behalf, wrote a letter to some gentile Christians needing reassurance and instruction in the faith. Let us now turn to the letter itself.

GOD'S PLAN AND THE BELIEVERS' PLACE IN IT

God has a plan that is being realized. The special message to the readers is that they have a secure place in God's unfolding purpose. Different terms describe the plan: it is a "mystery" (*mystērion,* 1:9), a "purpose" (*eudokian,* 1:9), a "counsel" (*boulē*, 1:11), a "plan" (*oikonomia*, 3:9). This plan is not some new idea; God has prepared it beforehand and it is in full accordance with his will (1:11). Though God's purpose was operative in the past, it was shrouded in mystery then. It has not been known by "sons of men in other generations" (3:5, cf. 3:9). This eternal purpose of God, hidden for ages, has come to a climax in Christ Jesus. That is the key. What was hidden is now disclosed. Furthermore, those who find themselves "in Christ," those who believe, are shown their place in God's plan and instructed concerning how to coordinate their lives with God's purpose. Their place in this grand plan is sealed by the "promised Holy Spirit" (1:13).

Two overriding purposes dominate the first half of the letter (chaps. 1–3): the faithful are assured of their secure place in God's purpose and are instructed concerning the consequences of this election. Throughout the opening chapters, the aorist, the tense of completed action in the past, prevails. The situation of the readers is *already* secured. God's action in Christ has made sure of that. God "has blessed us" (1:3). "He chose us" (1:4). "He destined us" (1:5). He "freely bestowed" his grace (1:6). "We have redemption" (1:7). "We . . . have been destined and appointed" (1:12). "You . . . were sealed with the promised Holy Spirit" (1:13) and therefore already have the downpayment (1:14) of what is to come.

Compared with the unquestionably Pauline letters, this drive to clarify what has already been accomplished for the believers will be most striking in Ephesians' claim that God "made us alive together with Christ . . . and raised us up with him" (2:5–6). Already alive together with Christ; already raised with him! In Philippians Paul is more guarded: "becoming like him in his death, that if possible I may attain the resurrection from the dead" (Phil. 3:10–11). There Paul does not question the believer's solidarity with Christ in his *death*, but sharing his resurrection is still a hope for the future. Rom. 6:5 makes the same temporal distinction found in Philippians: "For if we have been united with him in a death like his, we shall certainly be united with him in a resurrection like his." With Ephesians, however, the distinction collapses: the believers share with Christ not only his death but also his resurrection. They have been raised with him already.

Because of the immeasurable riches of God's grace, the readers are secure in Christ. They are caught up in God's plan. They have been transferred to a new situation. But no one should be misled to think that the believers may relax with nothing to do. In the "no longer . . . now" contrasts that are so typical of Ephesians (2:1 ff., 2:11 ff., 2:19, 4:14, 17, 5:8), the author provides the context for his admonition. They are no longer "strangers," without hope and without God (2:12). They are no longer "dead through the trespasses and sins in which you once walked" (2:1). "You must no longer walk as the gentiles do, in the futility of their minds" (4:17). With a shift of metaphor, the same point is made: "Once you were darkness, but now you are light in the Lord; walk as children of light" (5:8). The last statement—"walk as children of light"—shows that the author's purpose is not simply to compare their former situation with their new one. He is eager to instruct them concerning the life that is appropriate to their new status. The believers must now "walk" differently from before.

THE PROPER "WALK"

For Jews and gentiles in Jesus' times, "walk" was a widespread metaphor for the way one lived. To "walk" a certain way was to live in that manner. When one's situation changed, one "walked" differently. The recipients of Ephesians could understand very well when the second half of the letter opened with the appeal that the readers "walk worthy of the calling" (4:1). The RSV translators have adequately captured the sense of the old language when they render it "lead a life worthy of the calling."

The opening half of Ephesians (chaps. 1–3) describes God's now-revealed plan and assures the believers of their place in it; the second half of the letter (chaps. 4–6) instructs the readers concerning the "walk," the way of life, that is appropriate to the plan now under way in Christ. The theme that binds chapters 4–6 together is the "proper walk."

Paul's letters usually build toward an appeal section where the consequences of the claims concerning God's action in Christ are spelled out for the readers. A classic example is Rom. 12:1: "I appeal to you therefore, brethren, by the mercies of God, to present your bodies as a living sacrifice, holy and acceptable to God. . . ." Ephesians follows the same pattern: "I therefore, a prisoner of the Lord, beg [the Greek, *parakalō,* is the same as in Rom. 12:1] you to walk worthy of the calling to which you have been called" (Eph. 4:1). This suggests that there is a walk that is "unworthy," inappropriate. And sure enough, when the theme of "walking" next appears in Ephesians, the author says: "you must no longer walk as the gentiles do . . ." (4:17).

The theme of the "proper walk" punctuates chapter 5 as well. The chapter opens with the admonition "walk in love" (5:2). A few verses later, in a contrast between the children of light and the children of darkness, the author calls for the readers to "walk as children of light" (5:8). The theme is concluded with the generalizing point: "look carefully then how you walk" (5:15).

So in Ephesians, God's formerly hidden plan is disclosed to the faithful and their place in that plan is described as secure. By the commonplace idea of life as a "walk" the author schools the readers concerning the implications of God's purpose for the way they live. In sum, all the special features of the letter to the Ephesians must be seen against the background provided by these basic claims: God has a now-disclosed plan that he is carrying out. The believers are apprised of this plan and know that they have been included in it by God's grace. Finally, they must "walk," that is, lead their lives, in a way appropriate to God's plan and their place in it. We turn to an examination of some special features of the letter.

THE VARIED IMAGES OF THE CHURCH
IN EPHESIANS

As the centuries have passed readers of Ephesians have been struck by its idea of the church. In the Pauline letters such as Philemon and Galatians, Christians everywhere may be referred to as "brothers" together, or as the "saints" of God. But Paul lacks an overarching use of the term "church" to suggest a bond of Christians in one place with those in another. For Paul Christians in different locales belong to one another, but the term "church" is never used by him to suggest that overall unity of life or purpose. For Paul "church" signifies the worshiping believers as they gather together. The groups of Christians scattered over the Roman province of Galatia, for example, are addressed as "the *churches* of Galatia" (Gal. 1:2).

Like the Pauline letters, Ephesians knows that it is "the saints who are also faithful in Christ Jesus" (1:1) who are brought together into community with one another as a result of "the immeasurable riches of his grace in kindness toward us in Christ Jesus" (2:7). The church is composed of all the "saints," those set apart for God. They are "members of the household of God" (2:19).

But there is a striking difference in Ephesians' view of the church compared with the Pauline letters. No longer are we simply dealing with "the church in your house" (Philem. 2). No longer do we confront the notion of "the churches in Galatia" (Gal. 1:2). In those phrases, the church is localized. The worshiping faithful are the church and there may be one such "church" gathering in someone's house in one place or there may be different groups, "churches," of such people meeting across an entire Roman province. Ephesians does not share such a view of "church" and "churches," a fact that becomes clear the very first time the term "church" appears. Eager to stress what has already been accomplished in Christ, the author of Ephesians sets up the universe, the cosmos, as the only vista against which the truly massive proportions of God's plan can be appreciated. Christ has been raised by God and made to "sit at his right hand in the heavenly places" (1:20). That position insures his dominion over "all rule and authority and power" (1:21). The same point is reaffirmed in the next verse, by utilizing the language of the Psalms: God "has put all things under his [Christ's] feet" (1:22). The mention of "feet" triggers the fertile mind of the author and the same assertion is made again, this time using the metaphor of "head": God "has made him [Christ] the head over all things for the church" (1:22). The first explicit mention of the "church" in Ephesians, therefore, comes in a context where the author portrays the cosmic significance of God's action in Christ. God has raised Christ to power in the heavenly places, far above all rival and contending powers. And all of this bears directly on the church. The dominion over all things granted by God to Christ has the church as its object. The first mention of "church" in Ephesians sets it in the context of God's great plan that is being worked out in the cosmos, in the entire universe.

As the letter unfolds, this picture is confirmed. The church is the beneficiary of God's cosmic plan that is taking shape, and it has a task appropriate to that plan. The "God who created all things" (3:9) now discloses "what is the plan of the mystery hidden for ages" (3:9), namely, "that through the church the manifold wisdom of God might now be made known to the principalities and powers in the heavenly places" (3:10). God's purpose is unfolding *for* the church (she is its beneficiary) and *through* the church (she is the agent by which the plan is disclosed). The church's task is on a scale with God's purpose of which it is so directly a part. As the plan is cosmic in proportions, so is the church. The church that Ephesians describes is therefore not simply the localized gathering of worshiping believers who meet in someone's home. It includes those persons, but views them on a grander scale as the agents who disclose God's purpose—even in the heavenly places (3:10). Accordingly, the plural, "churches," would be absolutely inappropriate to Ephesians and is never found there.

Against the vista provided by this cosmic backdrop, the author of Ephesians develops an exceedingly rich view of the church through his creative use of various images and metaphors. A brief examination of the primary images of the church will help us see the multi-faceted portrait Ephesians offers.

The Body of Christ

The "body of Christ" is Ephesians' best known and most pervasive metaphor for the church. Beginning with 1:22 the church is explicitly identified as the "body of Christ" and the motif continues through most of the letter.

As a way of assessing the prominence of this image in Ephesians we may observe that the indisputably authentic Pauline letters do not frequently resort to this image. Ephesians and many popular modern representations of Paul play up the importance of the body of Christ. Among the Pauline letters only Romans 12 and 1 Corinthians 12 develop the "body of Christ" metaphor (cf. Rom. 7:4; 1 Cor. 10:16). In both cases the image is introduced in the interest of reaffirming Christian unity.

In Ephesians, however, the body of Christ image is used sweepingly across the document and serves four major functions. First, and basically, it allows the author to explain how the believers relate to Christ. As with the unquestioned Pauline letters, so in Ephesians the believers are "in Christ." The author of Ephesians uses the "body of Christ" terminology as a way of declaring and developing that central Pauline claim. As a result, the closely related phrases, "in Christ" and "in the body of Christ" are used interchangeably (cf. 2:15–16). Apparently the author of Ephesians can assume that his readers do not need to be convinced of this, but understand it already. Nowhere does he try to persuade them of its truth; rather, the claim that "we are members of his body" (5:30) is made in so matter-of-fact fashion that it is a fixed point from which to reason. The "body of Christ" terminology in Ephesians helps the author develop for his readers the implications of their being "in Christ." They are members of Christ's body.

Second, the "body of Christ" image helps the author express the way that the individual believers belong to one another and should relate to one another. As a body has many members (cf. 1 Cor. 12:12), it follows that the different members of the same body are members of one another (4:25). Accordingly the believers are to live together in unity. Like any healthy body, the different members ought to build one another up. Love is the means. The body of Christ upbuilds itself in love (4:16). When there is unity and when the diverse gifts of Christ are functioning as they should, the body of Christ is edified (4:12).

The author of Ephesians can extend the metaphor and make the same point. When all the members are functioning together as they should, when the different gifts are operative, the body of Christ is built up until all attain mature manhood. Childhood is left behind. A construction metaphor, "edification," has given way to an image of growth, but the point is the same. The body of Christ, when properly in unity, grows, is built up. In fact, the author says as much: "speaking the truth in love, we are to grow up in every way into him who is the head, into Christ, from whom the whole body, joined and knit together by every joint with which it is supplied, when each part is working properly, makes bodily *growth* and *upbuilds* itself in love" (4:15–16).

In these two functions of the "body of Christ" terminology— to illuminate how Christians are related to Christ and how Christians belong to each other—Ephesians is very much in line with the use of the same image in 1 Corinthians 12 and in Romans 12. But there is a third way that Ephesians uses the body of Christ image—and that usage is found nowhere in the undisputed Pauline letters. According to Ephesians, not only are the faithful members of Christ's body members of the church, but Christ is the "head" of that body, the church. In Ephesians Christ is not simply equated with his body; he is also "head" of that body. The Christians are at once "in Christ" and at the same time enjoined "to grow up in every way into him who is the head, into Christ" (4:15). As head of his body, the church, Christ is the *goal* towards which the growth of the body must aspire. In the remainder of the same sentence the matter is turned around and viewed from another perspective. Christ, the head, is also the *source* of the power that enables bodily growth: "from whom the whole body, joined and knit together by every joint with which it is supplied, when each part is working properly, makes bodily growth and upbuilds itself in love" (4:16). When the church as the body of Christ recognizes Christ, its head, as its goal (4:15) and its source (4:16), then bodily growth and edification take place.

Implicit in this notion of Christ as head of his body, the church, is a necessary submission of the body to the head. In this regard, what is implicit through much of the letter is directly expressed in the household code addressed to wives (5:22 f.). There wives are urged to be submissive to their husbands "as to the Lord" (5:22). The rationale for such submission is found in the analogies or parallels the author sees between the wife's relation to her husband and the church's relation to Christ. "For the husband is the head of the wife as Christ is the head of the church, his body" (5:23). The church must be submissive to its Lord, its head.

When compared with the notion of the body of Christ in Romans 12 and 1 Corinthians 12, Ephesians represents an innovation: Christ is the head of his body, the church. In sum, the author of Ephesians capitalizes on the image of the head in three complementary ways: the head, Christ, is the goal towards which the body, the church, should live; the head is the source by which the body may achieve growth; and the head is Lord over the body and consequently the body, the church, must be submissive to it.

The fourth major function of the body of Christ image in Ephesians is to help the faithful understand their place in the universe, the cosmos. The "body of Christ" terminology is introduced first near the conclusion of the heavily christological section, 1:3–23, whose core affirmations are that God "has put all things under his [Christ's] feet and has made him the head over all things for the church, which is his body" (1:22). Whether the terminology be that Christ is "head over" all things or that all things are "put under his feet," the point is the same: Christ is Lord over all. In 1:10, Ephesians declares that God has "a plan for the fullness of time, to unite [literally, "to head up"] all things in him [Christ], things in heaven and things on earth." Christ's cosmic "heading up" of all things, whether in heaven or on earth, is for the sake of the church, Christ's body (1:22). The church as the body of Christ has a special place in God's plan for his whole creation, the universe. Accordingly, the church has a role in the cosmic Lordship of Christ over all things.

This "body language" of Ephesians is common coinage in the Graeco-Roman world and would have been readily understood by the gentiles to whom Ephesians is apparently directed. The Stoics, for example, made considerable use of the body metaphor as a way of describing social groupings. The people in the social group were the members of the body. Even the universe could be viewed as a body, an organic whole, with each person understood as a member of that body. Under the Roman emperor Nero (A.D. 54–68), the empire was referred to as Nero's body, and in some ways like Ephesians, Nero was said to be the head of his body, the empire. Ephesians' use of the terminology is not peculiar when viewed against the background of the Graeco-Roman world, but rather provides a ready means for the author to convey important points about Christ and the church to his gentile audience.

The Bride of Christ

One of the most intriguing images for the church in early Christianity portrays her as bride to Christ, the groom. Jesus' own sayings speak of bridal banquets (Luke 14:8 ff.; Matt. 22:1 ff.) and bridegrooms (Matt. 25:1 ff.), and some sayings even seem to refer to him as the bridegroom (Mark 2:19–20, Matt. 9:15, Luke 5:34–35). In 2 Corinthians Paul refers to himself as the "best man" who has prepared the church as the bride for Christ (11:2). But the image is never developed in the NT apart from the Book of Revelation (19:6–10) and Eph. 5:21–33.

The idea of a divine marriage is certainly not the invention of the early church; nor is it even a construction of ancient Israel, though she certainly knew about it. In fact, it is an archaic image present in the oldest evidence from the ancient Near East where the conviction was that gods and goddesses formed marriages together. From such a distant past, Israel inherited the notion and applied it at several points in the prophetic literature to Israel and Yahweh, her God. Ezekiel speaks of the youngster that Yahweh found in the wilderness and nursed into a beautiful maiden whom he took for his wife (Ezekiel 16). The young woman is identified as Jerusalem (16:3), representing Israel. Ezekiel tells the story so that he can report on her subsequent whoring with others, that is, her unfaithfulness to Yahweh (16:15

ff.). Hosea picks up much the same idea, though he devotes no time to Israel's youth. He moves directly to portray Israel as an unfaithful wife to Yahweh. Elsewhere in Israel's traditions, the Song of Songs is replete with language of two lovers committed to each other, material that already in early rabbinic times was understood allegorically of Yahweh and Israel. That rich mine of images lay open before the early Christians in the very scriptures they shared with Israel. It is not surprising that the Christians took over the imagery and with slight modification applied it to Christ and the church.

Ephesians shares with most of the older divine marriage accounts three identifiable traits or emphases: 1) the bride must be free of all blemishes and defects since they would detract from her beauty; 2) she must be dowried, and she is clothed in that dowry so that she is resplendent; and 3) she must appear before the groom, prepared for the consummation of the marriage.

Ephesians recognizes that the cleansing and purifying of the church as Christ's bride has taken place because of Christ's love and death for her: "Christ loved the church and gave himself up for her, that he might sanctify her, having cleansed her by the washing of water with the word" (5:25–26). Accordingly, she is without blemish or defect that would diminish from her splendor. Not only did he purify her—in Ephesians, that is an action completed in the past—but Christ continues in the present to nourish and care for her: "For no man ever hates his own flesh, but nourishes and cherishes it, as Christ does the church" (5:29).

What was done in the past—the cleansing, the purifying by Christ's death—establishes the church in the present when she is nourished and cherished by Christ, and leads toward an event in the distant future. All that has been done for the church and all that is currently being done for her point to the great moment in the future when the bride, properly cleansed and endowed with purity, will be presented to Christ. The anticipated consummation of marriage is tantamount to judgment. "Christ loved the church and gave himself up for her . . . that the church might be presented before him in splendor, without spot or wrinkle or any such thing, that she might be holy and without blemish" (5:25–

27). What is the church's dowry as she stands before Christ? Her "splendor" of purity and holiness. Stated in negatives, it is her being without blemish, without spot, wrinkle, or anything that might detract from that holiness.

The concern with holiness and purity of the bride touches upon a larger theme in Ephesians. From the beginning of the letter this note has been sounded: the readers have been chosen "before the foundation of the world" (1:4), and they are moving toward the judgment-presentation of the bride before the groom. From before all time until the end of time—these are the borders of God's purposes with the faithful. "He chose us in him before the foundation of the world, that we should be holy and blameless before him" (1:4). The word translated "blameless" (*amōmos,* literally "without blemish") is the same term that appears—again linked with "holy"—in the passage that anticipates the presentation of the bride before Christ (5:27): "that she might be holy and without blemish [*amōmos*]." Though the word translated "without blemish" occurs in Ephesians only in 1:4 and 5:27, the related and positively stated concern with holiness is a strong motif throughout the letter (1:1, 4, 13, 15, 18; 2:19, 21; 3:5, 8, 18; 4:12, 30; 5:3, 27; and 6:18). In Ephesians as in the Pauline letters, to be "holy" or a "saint"—the Greek word (*hagios*) is the same for both—is to be set apart for God on the basis of God's initiative. It is God who makes saints by the free gift of his grace and love. Absent is the distortion that "saints" are those who have achieved a certain level of sanctity by performance of good deeds and avoidance of "sins."

In these Ephesians verses portraying the church as the bride of Christ (5:22–33), the concern with blemishes merits one more observation. Deepseated in the scriptures of Israel are extensive regulations concerning the condition of the creatures to be offered in sacrifice to God. These guidelines prohibited anyone from sacrificing a lame, sick, or otherwise decrepit animal under the guise of fulfilling one's obligations to God. The code word that recurs in those injunctions is "blemish"; the animals must be without blemish of any kind. At some point in Israel's life, the concern with "blemishes" was imposed as a standard by which to

judge the purity expected of priests (Lev. 21:17 ff.). The author
of Ephesians inherits this pervasive concern for purity and applies it to the church as Christ's bride (cf. Deut. 24:1). The
church is to be presented to Christ as his pure bride. The ancient
divine marriage idea demands that the bride be presented in
splendor. Ephesians defines that "splendor" positively—"holy";
and negatively—"without blemish." Together the two words,
"holy" and "blemishless," mirror the author's pervasive concern
for the church. The church must live in the holiness appropriate
to God's grace; the church must "walk" in such a way that it
avoids any blemishes that would mar her purity.

The author of Ephesians has chosen a striking point at which
to introduce the "bride of Christ" metaphor. It appears in the
opening set of addresses to husbands and wives in the household
code (5:21–6:9). The sacred marriage of Christ and the church
is carefully interwoven with the author's admonitions to the wife
and the husband. Human marriage has been raised to lofty
heights by the very association, though many will feel certain
features of the author's depiction of the role of the wife "unac-
ceptable for today." Nevertheless, the author's point is that the
core of the family or household is the husband and wife. When
they live in the proper relation to one another they mirror God's
larger plans and purposes. In fact, we should put it even more
directly. When husband and wife relate as they should, they
make real in the human family God's cosmic purposes in Christ.
No wonder the author of Ephesians can tell his readers they were
formerly homeless but now are members of the household of God
(2:19)!

The Household of God

In the times when Ephesians was written, the basic sociological
unit was not the limited family of today: two parents and their
offspring. Instead, the fundamental social organization was the
household, and it was composed not only of parents and children,
but also of slaves. The tangle of relationships in such a household
included not only husbands/wives, parents/children and children/
children, but also the relation of the slaves to the rest of these

people. The author of Ephesians employs "household" and "family" as interchangeable social metaphors to describe the new situation in which the believers find themselves. Under God the Father, the faithful have become "beloved children" (5:1), "children of light" (5:8). Indeed they are described in the beginning of the letter as "sons" of God (1:5). The believers have been born into a new life, a new family (3:14). They have a new Father, and are guided by a different Spirit. As the author puts it succinctly, they are "members of the household of God" (2:19).

The analogy is extended. Just as sons of a regular family can expect a legacy, so the new children of God can anticipate an inheritance. There is one difference: the inheritance from God strains the language as the author tries to give it adequate expression. Nearly redundant phrases result including "riches . . . lavished upon us" (1:7–8), "the riches of his glorious inheritance" (1:18), and "immeasurable riches" (2:7). Categories of human experience almost prove inadequate.

The unity of the new family of God also finds expression through the metaphor of inheritance. The "mystery of Christ" (3:4) is disclosed: "Gentiles are fellow heirs" (3:6). The inheritance is open to all who are included in God's new family, whether they be Jews or gentiles.

There can be no distinction between Jew and gentile when God is the Father and expresses his power over all families by giving them names. Every family on earth and in heaven is named by God the Father (3:14). God's power expresses itself across as vast and inclusive a scope as the mind can imagine—on earth and in heaven—to name all families and thereby to bring them together under him as Father. God is the Father of the faithful; the believers should live as the beloved children that they have become in Christ. As such they can be confident of their ultimate sharing in the great riches that make up their inheritance.

As in Ephesians there are two ways of "walking," so in terminology appropriate to the household, there are rival sonships, two different notions of childhood. The author reminds the readers that they "were children of wrath" just like everyone else (*hoi polloi,* 2:3; cf. 4:14). Christians are no longer to associate with the "sons of disobedience," a Semitic way of saying "disobedient people" (5:6; cf. 2:2). Once the readers were of the wrong sonship, but now they are properly children of God.

In terms akin to those employed in the Dead Sea Scrolls, the author sets the proper sonship over against the errant one. "Once you were darkness, but now you are light in the Lord; walk as children of light" (5:8). Once more the metaphor of the "walk" is intertwined with the proper sonship motif at the opening of chapter 5: "Therefore be imitators of God, as beloved children. And walk in love" (5:1-2).

So there are two walks, two sonships. The readers who walk as they should are living as the children of light, as God's beloved children. The matter is carried one step farther. There are two spirits. Though the discussion of the rival spirits that may govern one's life is not developed at length in Ephesians, it is present. The readers are reminded that they once "followed the spirit that works among the sons of disobedience" (2:2), but they now find themselves under the guidance of another spirit, the Holy Spirit. As believers in Christ, they have been "sealed with the promised Holy Spirit, which is the guarantee of our inheritance until we acquire possession of it" (1:13-14).

The different spirits lead in different directions. The children who follow the spirit that governs disobedience are children of wrath, children destined for wrath. The children who are sealed with the promised Holy Spirit have a radically different future. It includes an inheritance of incredible riches—and the promised Holy Spirit is the guarantee or downpayment (*arrobon*) of it (1:14). Rival "walks," rival "sonships," and rival "spirits." The faithful, those true sons who are sealed with the Holy Spirit and "walk" appropriately to their calling in Christ, are the ones who imitate God "as beloved children" (5:1) and walk in love (5:2) and aim for the inheritance proper to the true children of God. It is these faithful who make up the household of God.

Fellow Citizens With the Saints

In the world of the original readers of this letter, a larger social unit by which people normally identified themselves was the city,

city-state (*polis*), or province to which they belonged. Identity was in part disclosed by citizenship. One of the sterner penalties that could be imposed on an individual was exile. The author of Ephesians casts this image on a large scale, describing the readers' pre-Christian situation as one of being strangers, sojourners, aliens, wanderers (2:19). They had been persons without citizenship.

To describe their new situation in Christ, the author deftly turns the image around and declares that the faithful are now "fellow citizens with the saints" (2:19). Whereas before they were aliens, now they have citizenship, and the author uses a strong word, *sympolitai,* joint-citizens or fellow citizens, to affirm that the readers are now citizens on full parity with the saints. In fact they too are saints, as the author directly addresses them in the opening verse of the letter. The church is peopled with saints. What does it mean to belong in this Christian community? It is to have a special citizenship, a saintly one, in God's *polis,* God's state.

The church viewed as family and as a new citizenship are complementary pictures. Both images, though drawing from different social contexts, are used by the author to describe the new status of the faithful in Christ.

The Holy Temple

House metaphors and indeed construction images are well-known in the Pauline correspondence. For example, with the troublesome and unruly Corinthians, Paul used the notion of Christ as a foundation on which he and other people had built (1 Cor. 3:10–15; cf. Rom. 15:20).

In Ephesians the model of the "holy temple" emerges from a concatenation of images near the end of chapter 2. There proper citizenship merges into the notion of the household of God. The latter elicits the image of a structure, a building. The author of Ephesians uses that opportunity to describe nearly everything about this structure but the shape of the roof! What is the foundation? It is the prophets and apostles. What is the cornerstone? It is Christ Jesus himself. In Christ, "the whole structure is joined together and grows into a holy temple in the Lord" (2:21). Then, with somewhat cumbersome language, the author shows how the readers relate to that holy temple. In Christ they are built into the temple "for a dwelling place of God in the Spirit" (2:22).

Apart from 2:21, there is no other explicit mention of the "holy temple" in Ephesians. There may be one possible indirect reference to it, however. As chapter 3 moves towards its powerful conclusion, the author reports his prayer for the faithful. Themes first related to "temple" at the end of chapter 2 re-emerge near the end of chapter 3. The presence of the Spirit is important in both passages (2:22; 3:16). The temple as the "dwelling place of God" (2:22) is paralleled by the heart as the dwelling place of Christ in the inner man (3:17). The "foundation" of the holy temple in chapter 2 is the prophets and apostles (2:20); at the end of chapter 3 the author prays that the readers may have a certain power because they are "rooted and grounded in love" (3:17). The word "grounded" there is the same as the term for "foundation" in 2:20. One final point of possible connection with the "holy temple" metaphor appears in chapter 3: because the readers have their foundation properly established on love, the author prays that they "may have power to comprehend with all the saints what is the breadth and length and height and depth" (3:18). But of what? What is it of which the readers are to know the measurements? From Numbers through Amos (7:7 f.) through to the Book of Revelation (11:1 ff.), there is an enduring set of traditions that the temple—or at least Jerusalem—is measured or gauged. Clearly in Revelation the measuring of the temple and the altar and the people who worship there is suggestive of judgment. How does the temple measure up to its calling? It is possible here in Ephesians that the author's prayer portrays the believers as built on the proper foundation and accordingly knowing the parameters of their new dwelling.

One New Man in Place of the Two

In terms appropriate to Israel, 2:11 opens with an address to "you gentiles," reminding the readers that they were once aliens from the "commonwealth of Israel and strangers to the covenants of promise" (2:12). Borrowing further from Israel (cf. Isa. 57:19 and Zech. 6:15) the author describes how in Christ those "far off have been brought near" (2:13). The "dividing wall of hostility" (2:14) has been broken down. The both (*ta amphotera,* "the two" or "all," if there are more than two) have become one (2:14). Given the context, those "far off" and those "near" are intended; they have become one. Gentiles and Jews are made one. Peace has been preached to both. Then, using categories not derived from Israel, the author seizes another way of expressing his point—and it may have been a way that gentiles could have understood quite well at that time: Christ creates in himself "one new man in place of the two" (2:15). The author's point is developed further in the next verse: "and [Christ] might reconcile us both to God *in one body* . . ." (2:16). With that the image of "one new man" phases into the "body" image already noted. Whether it is the "one new man" or the "body of Christ," the author affirms the unity of Jews and gentiles in the church.

In this section, we have seen that the author of Ephesians uses a wealth of images and metaphors to make his claims about the church and its place in God's plan. We now turn to other major features of the letter to the Ephesians.

ADMONITIONS FOR THE HOUSEHOLD

From the time of Aristotle, there were codes of household duties, tables that suggested the proper attitudes and responsibilities for each of the groups that made up households. Among other things, these tables or codes laid down the ways different people in the household should relate to the other members of it. From the culture around them, some early Christians took over the tables of instruction and guidance, the social codes of the times. To be sure, Christians rarely coopted any tradition or practice without adapting it to their new understanding of their situation in Christ and before God. Thus the household codes underwent modification and alteration in varying degrees.

The later literature of the NT incorporates several of these household codes. In Ephesians, the code is lengthy, extending from 5:21 through 6:9. Every other NT example of the code is more concise (Col. 3:18–4:1; 1 Pet. 2:18–3:7; cf. 1 Tim. 2:8–12; 6:1–2 and Tit. 2:1–10).

The author of Ephesians addresses each group of individuals in the households separately and directly: wives (5:22 ff.), husbands (5:25 ff.), children (6:1 ff.), fathers (6:4), slaves (6:5 ff.) and masters (6:9). Whereas the material in chapter 4 and the early part of 5 had instructed the faithful how they were to live with one another in the church, the material in the household code (5:21–6:9) instructs them how as Christians they ought to relate to one another in the household. Their daily lives together are to reflect their new life in Christ. The most fully developed section of the Ephesians code is that devoted to wives and husbands (5:22–33). In those verses the author shows in detail that the relationship of the husband and wife in the household should be patterned on the relationship of Christ and the church. The dominant figures within the household are to be transparent to God's cosmic purposes in Christ and the church. It is not just marriage that is being cast in a very positive light here; it is the relationship of the two lead figures of the family that reflects into the societal unit of the household the relationship of Christ and the church. The family is in continuity with God's purpose on a larger scale. One does not live one way in the church and another in one's household. In many respects the household is the microcosm of God's larger purposes, though the social unit is smaller and more intimate.

THE ESCHATOLOGY OF EPHESIANS

In the narrowest sense, eschatology is the study (*logos*) of the last things or end times (*eschaton*). According to this restricted view, a judgment or final reckoning is expected at the end of history. A verdict will be passed on an individual's life, and his ultimate destiny will depend on the way the verdict comes out. We know from the authentic Pauline letters, for example, that Paul anticipated he would be judged whether he carried out his call properly (1 Cor. 4:1–5; 9:24–27). The idea is widespread in early Christianity: all people will appear before the judgment seat of God or of Christ. At that point their lives, their "walks," will be evaluated (cf. Matt. 25:31 ff.).

Ephesians lacks this explicit picture of a judge who will pass verdicts on persons' lives, but it affirms the general idea. There are two differences. First, the immediacy of judgment is missing. Second, the judicial metaphors give way to other images preferred by the author. Ephesians calls for the readers to "be holy and blameless before him" (1:4). That is the terminology that traditionally belongs to the picture of a judge rendering verdicts at the consummation of history. We know from the remainder of Ephesians that the courtroom situation is not present. In its place is the assertion that the church, as Christ's betrothed, will be presented before him. The juristic tone is diminished as courtroom gives way to bridal chamber. The relation between judged and judge is formal, dreadful, and distant; that between bride and her groom is infinitely more intimate and secure. In a letter so concerned to reassure and encourage, the marriage metaphor preserves a sense of future judgment but "domesticates" it. The church, once purified by Christ's love and death for her, must remain that way until she is presented before him, "without spot or wrinkle or any such thing, that she might be holy and without blemish" (5:27).

Toward the end of the letter, the author makes much the same point, though the image is radically shifted from marriage to warfare (6:10 ff.). With the marriage of Christ and the church, the chief question at the presentation is purity. The church must be holy and without blemish. In the battle (6:10 ff.), the main issue is survival: "and having done all, to stand" (6:13). To be found standing when the cosmic battle is over is to survive the final judgment.

We must conclude that the early Christian metaphor that is frequently employed for the last times, a great judgment scene, is not present in Ephesians, but the same point is conveyed via other images. As the bride must be spotless when she is presented before the groom, so the victorious warrior is found standing when the battle is completed. In both of these instances, the requisite conditions are given to the faithful, not earned by them. The purity expected of the bride, the church, is made possible by Christ's loving death. Withstanding the great battle between God and the powers opposed to him is not accomplished by military training and cunning. It is made possible by the armament (*panoplia*) of God that is available to the faithful on the basis of prayer (6:18). God's armament is given to the ones who pray; without that armament survival is impossible.

In the course of downplaying the judicial picture of judgment at the end of history, the author of Ephesians has adopted a broader sense of eschatology. He is not concerned with the "last things" for their own sake. Nor is he committed to any sense of the immediacy of the "last things." He asks instead: how does that future inform the lives the believers should live in the present? A broader sense of eschatology is at work in Ephesians. The believers must live in the knowledge that they will someday be presented as the bride before Christ. They live with an eye to the future in hopes of retaining their purity and blemishlessness given to them in the past and retained in the present. They prayerfully prepare for the battle by asking for God's strength in the present. Insofar as the future is important in Ephesians, it serves to emphasize the present.

Everything that we have thus far discussed about Ephesians' eschatology has appropriately been in temporal categories of past, present, and future. But in Ephesians the categories of time are supplemented by unusually heavy dependence on notions of space. Consider, for example, the very fitting end of the first half of the letter (3:14 ff.). God's power is being celebrated. It is the author's prayer that his readers "may have power to comprehend with all the saints what is the breadth and length and height and depth, and to know the love of Christ which surpasses knowledge" (3:18–19). Categories of power and space blend into one another as the author attempts to describe what finally defies full description. It is as if the words of Ephesians signal an overload on the communications that need to be borne. The result: categories overlap; metaphors mix; thoughts pile up. Temporal expressions—as in past, present, and future—do not suffice to indicate the enormity of God's grace at work in his plan. Spatial categories take center stage.

Some of the Pauline assertions that are regularly made by using temporal assertions are transposed in Ephesians into concepts of space. The peculiar spatial interest of Ephesians is nowhere better seen than in the central christological claim of chapter 1 and its development in chapter 2. Drawing heavily on Psalm 110 and Psalm 8, the author of Ephesians fashions his fundamental affirmation concerning Christ: God "raised him from the dead and made him sit at his right hand in the heavenly places" (1:20). Resurrection and ascension terminology are fused. As a consequence of God's exalting Christ, Christ is "far above all rule and authority and power and dominion" (1:21). The same point is expressed differently in the next words: "He has put all things under his feet and has made him the head over all things" (1:22). Christ's exaltation and Lordship are expressed in spatial categories.

The opening part of chapter 2 applies those christological assertions to the readers. The God who raised Christ from the dead and made him sit at his right hand in the heavenly places has "made us alive together with Christ . . . and raised us up with him, and made us sit with him in the heavenly places in Christ Jesus" (2:5-6). Christ was raised; the believers are raised with him. Christ was made to sit at God's right hand in the heavenly places; the believers sit with him, secure in that place of power and authority. The same root verbal ideas are present when applied to Christ and when applied to the believers. The believers' solidarity with Christ is expressed by reusing the same words in both places. In chapter 2, the actions of the verbs are completed in the past. As a result, the present status of the believers is that they currently sit with Christ—already at the right hand of God in the heavenly places.

Elsewhere in the letter, spatial categories are used to express the readers' previous alienation and their new, secure situation in Christ. Such a notion is found in the construction "separated from Christ" (*chōris Christou*, 2:12) and is highlighted in 2:13: "now in Christ Jesus you who once were far off have been brought near in the blood of Christ." Likewise in 2:17: "And he came and preached peace to you who were far off and peace to those who were near." Expressing the same idea, but using categories from a different sociological circumstance, the author moves directly to apply his spatial claims once more: "you are no longer strangers (*xenoi*) and sojourners (*paroikoi*)" (2:19). Both *xenoi* and *paroikoi* suggest persons who are exiled from their home country, separated from their own place. The faithful may continue to be strangers or aliens in the world in some sense, but their true citizenship is secure because they sit with Christ at the right hand of God in the heavenly places.

The author's point is basically the same whether he employs temporal claims—"he chose us in him before the foundation of the world" (1:4) or spatial ones—"you who once were far off have been brought near in the blood of Christ" (2:13). His rich use of spatial categories supplements and sometimes slightly modifies the more traditionally temporal assertions about what has been accomplished in Christ.

THE MOVEMENT OF EPHESIANS

Interpreters of Ephesians have readily noted the way in which the conclusion of chapter 3, moving as it does towards the lofty praise of God's power and climaxing with the ascription of glory to God (3:21–22), divides the letter into two parts. The second half of the document (chaps. 4–6) concerns itself with the entreaty and instruction so typical of the concluding sections of Paul's letters (cf. Romans 12 and 1 Thessalonians 4). But the instruction of the faithful is not confined to the second half of Ephesians; it is already interwoven in chapters 1–3. To be sure, the emphasis does shift after chapter 3. There is more instruction afterwards than before. But in what follows we will suggest a much more fundamental and revealing movement in the letter to the Ephesians.

After the typical Pauline salutation (cf. Rom. 1:1–7; 1 Cor. 1:1–3; 2 Cor. 1:1–2; etc.), Ephesians opens with the broadest possible vista. The author moves from before the creation of the world (1:4) to the consummation of God's plan for the fullness of time (1:10). Temporally, his vision reaches beyond history in the past and to its culmination in the future. Spatially, the scope is equally grand, moving from the world (1:4) through the heavenly places (1:3), including "things in heaven and things on earth" (1:10). Such is the cosmic, universal scope in which the author introduces his understanding of God's plan.

God's plan for the fullness of time is to "head up" (*anakepha-laiōsasthai*) "all things" in Christ. The "all things" that are to be brought together in cosmic unity in Christ and under his power include "the things in heaven and the things on earth" (1:10). Broad vista indeed! The universe or cosmos is the arena where God's purposes are being realized.

Throughout the opening section (chaps. 1 and 2) the faithful are addressed and instructed concerning their place in God's eternal purpose: "that you may know what is the hope to which he has called you" (1:18). Though the readers are described as having been "dead through the trespasses and sins in which you once walked" (2:1–2) and "once separated from Christ" (2:11), they are now alive in Christ. The faithful are included in God's plan through Christ's exaltation above all rival and pretending powers. The faithful share Christ's exaltation (2:5–6) and thereby take their proper place in God's unfolding plan for the universe.

Thus the opening chapters of Ephesians set God's purposes in Christ against the backdrop provided by all of history and the universe itself. The place of the readers in history and in the universe is defined by their being "in Christ."

The first picture shown by the author of Ephesians is taken with a wide-angle lens. Nothing escapes the picture. Everything is included. The scope is vast. With chapter 3, however, it is as if the author has changed lenses and chooses to limit his scope a bit. What he gives up in breadth of view he gains in detail. Out of that vast first picture, the author chooses to focus on the believers and their role in God's plan. With that we move to the second picture.

This second, confined view depicts the readers and their place in God's purpose. They are not simply observers, passive by-standers in the cosmic drama. They are the community of be-

lievers, the church. And as the church they have a special role
to play. In chapter 3 we see that the church is given the task of
revealing God's plan to the powers that futilely contend with
God for the allegiance of God's own creatures (cf. 2:2). Whereas
the first picture was cosmic in scope, the second singles out the
church for closer viewing. Against the background provided by
God's cosmic purpose, the church's role as revelatory agent is
portrayed. It is noteworthy that the church's role is not confined
to the earth, but like God's plan of which it is so important a part,
the church plays a role not only in the earth but also in the
heavens where the "principalities and powers" may also be
found.

Much of the material in the remainder of chapter 3, all of
chapter 4 and some of chapter 5 has the church as its focus and
describes how the faithful are to comport themselves with one
another and in the world. For example, consider 5:5-7: "Be
sure of this, that no immoral or impure man, or one who is covet-
ous (that is, an idolater), has any inheritance in the kingdom of
Christ and of God. Let no one deceive you with empty words,
for it is because of these things that the wrath of God comes upon
the sons of disobedience. Therefore do not associate with them."

After the picture of the church is captured in such detail, the
author changes perspectives once more. The author of Ephesians
shifts the focus of his attention from the cosmos to the church in
the cosmos. Then, in an ever narrowing field of view, he turns his
attention to the next smallest social group of relevance for his
readers, the household, and presents his third picture.

The lives of the faithful within the household are marked by
God's plan as well. Their lives in the family must be attuned to
God's larger purposes; there is no dichotomy between life in
Christian community and conduct within the family. This could
not be clearer than when the author addresses the central pair
around which the household coalesces, the husband and the wife.
They are to relate to one another as Christ and the church relate.
The core relationship of the family, that of wife and husband, is
attuned to God's cosmic plan being realized in the universe
through Christ and the church. Likewise the other relationships

in the household must correspond to what is known about God and his purposes. Masters, for example, must relate to the slaves of the household "knowing that he who is both their Master and yours is in heaven, and that there is no partiality with him" (6:9).

Finally, in 6:10–20, the author makes his ultimate restriction of the scope and offers his fourth picture. His addresses individuals. As God's cosmic purpose unfolds, all of the faithful are to take upon themselves God's armament. It is God's battle that is to be won. The faithful must be active participants, but they do not provide their own armament. Ephesians is consistent: the power belongs to God. Here in the last section of the letter the author assures the readers that God's power is available to them. How do they gain access to that power here represented symbolically in terms of armament? The answer: "Pray at all times in the Spirit, with all prayer and supplication" (6:18). When the faithful prayerfully take on the "whole armor of God" (6:11), they will "be strong in the Lord and in the strength of his might" (6:10). They "will be able to stand against the wiles of the devil" (6:11). Availing themselves of God's power, the faithful will be found standing when the victory is accomplished. Those standing after the battle will be the heirs of God's riches that he makes available by his "plan for the fullness of time" (1:10).

The overall design or movement of Ephesians, therefore, begins with the cosmic depiction of God's plan, his purpose. Against the background provided by that description, the author examines the church and its role. Within the church the author sees the household as the next sub-unit. Finally he addresses the individuals concerning their responsibilities as they attune themselves to God's larger purposes. The movement of Ephesians is as follows:

God's cosmic plan	the church	the household	individuals

As the focus narrows step by step, the author does not discard any of the context provided by the previous stage or stages. In fact the author confirms the continuity of the Christian life in the total context of God's plan even though his portrayal of it narrows as the letter progresses.

There is one final, noteworthy detail. The author of Ephesians never resorts to stark or independent individualism. The community context of the life of faith is constantly in view. Even when describing the role of individuals (6:10–20), the "you" addressed is always the plural, never the singular. Furthermore, the prayer by which one dons the armor of God is not a self-serving prayer. It is a prayer "for all the saints" (6:18) and for the author (6:19). Even the prayer for the author is not directed to his personal welfare, but towards his bold proclamation of the gospel (6:19–20). That closing note ties the entire address to the individuals back into the living and proclaiming of the gospel which is in large measure the revealing of God's cosmic plan. So the final admonition to individuals (6:10–20) leads directly back to the opening concern with proclaiming God's great purposes for his faithful in the cosmos.

THE PLACE OF EPHESIANS IN EARLY CHRISTIANITY

Though it is unclear precisely when Ephesians was written, the letter does assume a place of importance in any effort to reconstruct the history and development of early Christianity. In at least three items Ephesians marks a shift from demonstrably earlier concerns and emphases.

1. Ephesians has lost the sense of the imminent end of the world that permeates so much of the earliest Christian writing. From Jesus (cf. Mark 9:1) to Paul (cf. 1 Thess. 4:13 ff.) there is the shared view: God's purposes will be consummated in a short time. Against this background Ephesians stands out in contrast. The end of the ages is not expected in the immediate future. In fact, categories of time take a back seat to categories of space. In Ephesians the faithful already sit with Christ at God's right hand in the heavenly places. The notion of the end of time pales in significance.

2. Tied inextricably to the decreased emphasis on time and the end of the world is an increased concern with how the faithful are to live with one another in the enduring world. The ethical admoni-

tions in the Pauline letters are not drawn up into a code or table of household duties as they are in Eph. 5:21–6:9. But as time passed Christians found themselves in need of practical counsel concerning how, in an enduring world, they should live, how they should "walk" in their households. In response, Ephesians has introduced an elaborated and "Christianized" version of the commonplace codes of household responsibilities.

3. Perhaps most strikingly, Ephesians represents a new understanding of the church when compared with the indisputably authentic Pauline letters. Gone is the "church in your house" model that we know from Philemon. In the place of the notion of churches as distinct groups of Christians, Ephesians uses the term "church" to refer to all Christians in the universe. In Ephesians the church is a cosmic entity, uniting Christians wherever they may be into one body, the body of Christ. Correspondingly, in Ephesians the mission of the church is understood to embrace not only the earth, but also the heavenly places. A universe-wide mission is appropriate to a cosmic church. In Ephesians we have both.

Whoever the author of Ephesians may have been he drew on Pauline traditions and applied them anew. In the process those traditions were sometimes reproduced, other times transformed in varying degrees. In a similar fashion, while we may not be able to discern a specific, historic crisis that elicited Ephesians, we can see that it is concerned to reassure the faithful, to instruct them concerning the proper "walk" in the world, to alert them to their responsibilities as individuals, as members of their own earthly households, and as members of the church in God's cosmic plan.

THE LETTER TO THE COLOSSIANS

The reader may recall that in 1961 at New Delhi during the Third Assembly of the World Council of Churches Joseph Sittler created an international sensation with his lecture on the "cosmic Christ." Using Col. 1:15–20, he asserted that in Christ nature and grace are one, so that salvation in Christ fills every corner of creation. Reaction to Sittler's use of 1:15–20 was often positive, but even more often negative.

In the last thirty years the whole letter to the Colossians has become a battleground. Against whom was the letter written? The Marcionite prologues already indicated that the key to an author's theology was to discover his opponents. Since the discoveries at Nag Hammadi and Qumran, theories about the identity of these opponents have increased. At present approximately fifty different theories exist, although, as is often the case, they fall easily into general categories. What pre-existing literary material did the author use in composing the letter? During the last thirty years a general consensus has been developing about the composition of the letter. How the letter was composed is another key to the author's theology. To be sure, it is particularly important in this letter to realize how theories about opponents influence theories about the composition of the letter and vice versa. Who wrote the letter? It is listed in Marcion's canon as Pauline, and Pauline authorship was never questioned until Mayerhoff in 1838; however, during these last thirty years scholars have increasingly abandoned the idea of Pauline authorship.

THE OPPONENTS AT COLOSSAE

The religious world of the time must not be thought of as a kind of pie, with each piece being a different religious persuasion.

Instead, that religious world was like a whirlpool, mixing the various religions and drawing them into its center, syncretism. Some distinct lines remained, some flotsam whirled in quasi-independence, but the pull was strong. "Normative Judaism" was not very normative. The distinction between Palestinian and Hellenistic Judaism has proven to be less than complete. Discoveries at Qumran and elsewhere indicate how syncretism had included Judaism. Who could help being caught up by this time? Magic, astrology, and the mystery religions were everywhere.

The famous Gnostic systems of Valentinus and Basilides will not appear until later, but the Gnostic "spirit" and "proto-Gnosticism" were already present. Thus it is no longer possible to juxtapose the Gnostic way of thinking and Hellenistic Judaism, as some have done; late Jewish speculation about Wisdom was made use of by those who were "proto-Gnostics."

What clues to opponents does the letter to the Colossians contain? The Colossians are endangered by "philosophy," which is linked with "empty deceit." That which is "according to human tradition" and the "elements" is contrasted with that which is "according to Christ" (2:8, 20, 22). Various "regulations" (2:14, 20) about food, drink, festivals, new moons, and sabbaths have been imposed upon the Colossians (2:16); certain things are not to be handled, tasted, or touched (2:21). Possibly circumcision was required (2:11–13). "Self-abasement" (2:18, 23), "severity to the body" (2:23), and perhaps "putting off the body of flesh" (2:11) indicate ascetic demands such as fasting. The "worship of angels," possibly "visions" and "self-abasement" (2:18), and "additional worship" (2:23) are descriptions of cultic requirements. Probably "fullness" (1:19; 2:9), "powers," and "principalities" (2:10, 15) refer to concepts held by the opponents at Colossae. On the periphery is terminology such as "wisdom" and "knowledge" (2:3), which may be used in a very normal sense, but which could reflect the opponents' usage.

Can this be equated with Judaism? The church at Colossae was itself made up of gentile Christians (1:21, 27; 2:13). It may be that the OT is implied in the letter, but it is never cited directly

except for the fragment: "seated at the right hand of God" (3:1).
The word "law" is never used, although the argument from silence
is not decisive.   Jewish is the keeping of regulations about food,
drink (wine), fasting, festivals, the new moon, and the sabbath.
It is doubtful, however, that the opponents demanded the rite of
circumcision, for this is not expressly noted, nor does the author
expressly warn against it; instead, circumcision here (2:11-13)
should be understood metaphorically.   More difficult are "visions"
and the "worship of angels" (2:16, 18).   However, some groups
within contemporary Judaism did write of visions which come with
the help of angels and which are about days, months, and sabbaths (Jub. 4:15-18).   The "worship of angels" by men is of
course impossible for a Jew.   It could mean the worship which
angels do, yet in 2:23 the "worship" is what men do, and the
ferment which syncretism was producing within Judaism, particularly at certain locations and among the lower classes, included the cult of angels.   Since this is not Judaism in the general
sense of the term, how should the opponents be described?

Are they like the Jewish sect at Qumran?   Already in 1875
J. B. Lightfoot theorized that the Colossian opponents had some
connection with the Essene community.   The Qumran community
was rigorous in its ethical and cultic observances and did speculate
about angels.   There is no indication, however, that at Qumran
angels were worshiped, but only that all members of the community joined the angels in the eternal worship the angels performed.   The whole family of words for "fullness" (1:19; 2:9) is
lacking at Qumran.   Most of all, the radical adherence to the law
which is found at Qumran has no parallel among the opponents
at Colossae, where the "regulations" (2:14, 20) are to serve the
"elements" (2:8, 20), not the law.

Are the opponents Gnostic?   Gnostics were often ascetic in
lifestyle and speculative in their thinking.   The opponents at
Colossae were similar.   Except for the letters to the Colossians
and Ephesians the term "fullness" in a technical sense is found
for the first time among the Gnostics, who speculated about the
"fullness" of God.   Later Gnosticism understood the "fullness"
to be the heavenly fullness to which God himself did not belong,

but in 1:19 and 2:9 the "fullness" is identical with God, an important difference. The Gnostic boasts of "wisdom" and "knowledge" (1:28, 2:3), but it is difficult to determine how much this was true at Colossae. On the other hand, the radical dualism which marks the Gnostic spirit is not present. The Gnostic has been saved from the created world through his own self-knowledge and would not worship angels (2:18), themselves created beings. In 1 Corinthians Paul battled a libertine form of Gnosis, but here the battle is with an ascetic form.

Jewish speculation centering on the Wisdom of God is another possibility. Wisdom was created at the beginning, before the world (Sir. 24:9, Prov. 7:22; cf. Col. 1:15, 18). Wisdom was with God at creation (Prov. 8:31; cf. Col. 1:16). She is the maker of "all things" (Wis. Sol. 7:22; cf. Col. 1:15-20). She is "an unspotted mirror of the working of God," "an image of his goodness" (Wis. Sol. 7:26; cf. Col. 1:15). To be sure, Jewish speculation identified Wisdom with the law (Sir. 24:22-23), which was not the case among the opponents at Colossae. Even closer are the Wisdom parallels found in Philo, who reflects contemporary Hellenistic Judaism.

But the over-arching syncretism of the time is an inescapable factor. The "elements" (2:8, 20) are also found in Gal. 4:3, 9, along with regulations about the calendar, and some sort of connection undoubtedly existed between the meaning of the term in both places, although that does not mean that the opponents are the same. Are the "elements" personal, angelic powers which are to be worshiped (2:18)? Originally the "elements" were the traditional earth, water, air, and fire. Only in the second century after Christ did the term "elements" by itself mean angelic powers. Within the NT lists of "principalities and powers" the "elements" are never included (1:16; 2:10). The "elements" are "human tradition" (2:8) and "regulations" (2:20). They have a certain kind of power because they are binding, but nothing in the context or in the parallel passages in Galatians demands that they be personified or identified with "angels" (2:18). At Colossae and at this point in history the relationship between the "elements" and "angels," "principalities," and "powers" had not been systematized. Schweizer refers to a Pythagorean text from the first century before Christ (Diels I 448, 33–451, 19) in which everything held by the Colossian opponents is present except the regulations about drink and the sabbath, and regulations about wine are found in related texts. The "elements," which are neither personified nor equated with angels, must be kept in balance, for when they are not, changes occur in the times of the day and the seasons. In order to escape this continuously changing world below and reach the eternal world above, the believer must gain the help of demons or the souls of heroes (the equivalent of angels) by venerating the gods and heroes, by purificatory washings, and by abstaining from sexual activity and from certain foods.

The opponents may have been connected with a mystery religion, in which, through ascetic practices and through secret rites of initiation, such as sacred meals or sacred marriages, believers were united with the god or goddess in order to escape the present evil world. In Phrygia, a part of central Asia Minor which includes Colossae, was the cult of the god Sabazios, and some of the Jews combined Jahweh, the God of Sabaoth, with Sabazios. Even though in the major Pauline letters the term "mystery" (1:27; 2:2) must be understood on the basis of apocalyptic, at Colossae the term would immediately be heard with overtones of the mystery cult. The "worship of angels" (2:18, 23) and "visions" (2:18) very probably imply a kind of initiation such as is found in the mystery religions.

Thus the Colossian opponents were syncretistic Jews infected with the Gnostic spirit. Colossae was situated in the Lycus valley near an important junction of roads leading to Ephesus, Smyrna, Syria, and the Euphrates valley, hardly an isolated corner of the Hellenistic world. Also, since every religious concept is modified to some degree when it is taken up and used in a new religious environment, the kind of interchange of ideas which took place at Colossae would lead to the conclusion that what can be determined about the meaning of religious concepts elsewhere cannot be applied directly to what religious concepts meant at Colossae. The situation was fluid. Yet it would be too vague merely to call the opponents syncretistic. On the other hand, it would be too

limiting to use only one or two of the categories above to describe
them. Probably it will never be possible to know exactly who they
were.

An additional difficulty in determining the teaching of the
opponents is that the author of the letter to the Colossians did
not know the Colossians directly (1:4, 7–9; 2:1). However, he
is very concerned and even personally involved; the letter is really
a kind of dialogue, as the twisting and turning of his argument
shows. At one point he praises them, rejoicing in "the firmness of
your faith in Christ" (2:5; cf. 1:4). To be sure, some are waver-
ing or have compromised, and he becomes polemic, as in the contrast he draws between "empty deceit" and "in him dwells the
whole fullness of the deity bodily" (2:8–9), or in the denunciation
of those who are "not holding fast to the Head" (2:19). At other
times his tone is mocking, as when he describes those who submit
to regulations as being subject to "things which all perish as they
are used" (2:20–21), or when he says the opponents are "puffed
up" because they insist on certain cultic practices (2:18).

Since they would have to be able to understand whatever he
wrote, he would have to use the words and concepts of the
opponents, although the extent to which he did can only be
established in certain passages. For example, the word "humility"
occurs in 2:18, 23, and 3:12. In the first two cases the context is
cultic; it is not an attitude, but a certain kind of practice which the
opponents insist on. In 3:12 the meaning is the virtue "humility,"
and cultic practice is not meant at all. Thus in the first two cases
the terminology of the opponents is being used.

Did he cite material from the opponents because he agreed
with it, because he agreed in part but needed to modify it, or
because he wished to refute it? To begin with, he may have misunderstood his opponents. Moreover, he would of course use
material from his own point of view, already a kind of modification. His purpose in writing is to admonish, a kind of refutation.
Finally, he may have been closer to his opponents than the term
implies. While rejecting the opponents' ascetic regulations, he
nevertheless calls them "a shadow of what is to come" (2:16–17).
All in all, because a very personal dialogue is taking place in this

letter, only relative certainty about the theological position of the opponents is possible.

THE OUTLINE OF THE LETTER

The internal structure of a letter cannot be as rigorous as that of a chemical formula. In this case the letter to the Colossians follows the general Pauline structure: opening (sender, addressee, and benediction), thanksgiving and intercession, body, ethical application, and closing (greetings, signature, and benediction).

I) 1:1–11.   Introduction.
  A) 1:1–2.   Opening: Paul and Timothy send God's grace and peace to the Colossian saints.
  B) 1:3–8.   Thanksgiving for their faith and love in Christ.
  C) 1:9–11.   Intercession for their growth in Christ.
II) 1:12–2:23.   The theological foundation: Christ is Lord.
  A) 1:12–23.   The hymn to Christ.
    1) 1:12–14. Introduction to the hymn.
    2) 1:15–20. The hymn: Christ is Lord.
    3) 1:21–23. Application of the hymn.
  B) 1:24–2:5. The apostolic office, which proclaims the mystery, Christ is Lord.
    1) 1:24–29. In its universal application through Paul to the revelation of the mystery of Christ.
    2) 2:1–5.   In its concrete application to Colossae through Paul.
  C) 2:6–23.   Polemic application of the Lordship of Christ to the situation in Colossae.
    1) 2:6–7.   Thematic summary: since you are in Christ, live in him.
    2) 2:8–15. Polemic re-statement of the theological foundation: Christ is your Lord.
    3) 2:16–23. Polemic application to the concrete teachings of the opponents at Colossae.
III) 3:1–4:6.   The ethical application: live what you are in Christ.
  A) 3:1–4.   Thematic summary: since you have been raised with Christ, live in him.
  B) 3:5–17.   Therefore put off the old man and put on the new.
    1) 3:5–11.   What it means to put off the old.
    2) 3:12–17. What it means to put on the new.

C) 3:18–4:1.   Concrete application to life in the household.
D) 4:2–6.   Concrete directives about prayer and evangelism.
IV) 4:7–18.   Conclusion.
  A) 4:7–9.   Recommendations for Tychicus and Onesimus.
  B) 4:10–15.   Greetings.
  C) 4:16–17.   Instructions.
  D) 4:18.   Personal signature and benediction.

THE THEOLOGICAL ARGUMENT

The traditional opening (1:1–2) is not simply a formality. "Grace" and "peace" are truly present because the benediction comes from "God our Father." Paul alone is named "apostle." Timothy's authority is legitimatized by his association with Paul. The thanksgiving (1:3–8) is one sentence and actually continues beyond its formal bounds (1:12–14; 2:5; cf. 1 Thess. 1:2–3:10). The Colossians are praised for their faith, love, and hope (1:4–5). The well-known Christian triad of virtues has been modified so that hope stands at the climax. Faith is founded in hope, and hope is that which is "laid up for you in heaven." The author here expresses himself in a way which is well-established for Christians. Our hope is sure. But in a sense the eschatological dynamic of hope has been exchanged for its objective content. The objective emphasis comes out further in "the word of the *truth*, the gospel" (1:5), and "*understood* the grace of God in *truth*, as you *learned* it from Epaphras" (1:6–7). Epaphras is another guarantee for the gospel. He is "our beloved fellow servant," and thus shares in the authority of the apostle; he is a "faithful" minister "on our behalf." Both the context and the better manuscripts support the reading "on our behalf." Throughout the section thanks is given because the gospel has been bearing fruit in the whole world (1:6) and also among the Colossians (1:6; "love" 1:4, 8). The intercession (1:9–11) picks up many expressions from the thanksgiving, for example, "pray for you" (1:3, 9). "Knowledge," "wisdom and understanding" (1:9–10) indicate again how important objective content is for the author. To be sure, it is not completely objective, for it must result in "a life worthy of the Lord" and in "bearing fruit."

The Hymn to Christ

The section begins like a second thanksgiving (1:12–14). However, it is the introduction, the introit, to the hymn which follows. The terminology is not typically Pauline; for example, he never uses the "forgiveness of sins" except in citations. In a repetitive, quasi-liturgical style God's deliverance of his saints is praised. "Redemption, the forgiveness of sins" and the aorist tense in "qualified," "delivered," and "transferred" point to a single completed event, complete salvation and particularly baptism. The "kingdom of his beloved Son," a kingdom of "light," is contrasted with the "dominion of darkness." This absolute contrast, plus the phrase "share in the lot of the saints," reflects the same emphasis on the completed and objective gospel as above in 1:5–7. In 1:12 the more difficult reading "you" is found in the better manuscripts; the shift from "you" to "us" occurs again in 2:13.

The author put together this introit from materials well-known in the intertestamental period, as, for example, in Qumran and in the early Christian community. His purpose was to prepare for the hymn to Christ in 1:15–20; at the same time he quoted the hymn because it illustrated and supported the theological argument he was developing.

That there is a hymn in 1:15–20 is a relatively recent discovery, but at present this is generally accepted. Although Bengel had already pointed out the parallelism within these verses, Schleiermacher was the first to make use of this parallelism to indicate the uniqueness of 1:15–20. To be sure, the mistake made by many scholars has been to use this very parallelism in such a procrustean fashion that the essence of poetry has been violated. In Hellenistic Judaism poetry did not have to be absolutely regular. 1 Tim. 3:16 is an exception. Even though regularities exist, repetition and even redundancy are natural, especially in synthetic parallelism. Both in form and in content a poem, in this case a hymn, has its own kind of logic. Moreover, the author has a tendency to use parallelism throughout the letter. (For example, 1:3 and 9; 1:3 and 12; 2:11 and 12; 2:20 and 3:1.)

Nevertheless, 1:15–20 stands out as a fragment of a hymn. In contrast to the dialogical form of the rest of the letter indicated by the frequent use of the personal pronouns "we" and "you," they are lacking here. The tone is exalted and declaratory. Most of all, literary devices abound. The parallelism can be demonstrated to some degree even in English:

15a	Who is the image
18b	Who is the beginning
15b	the first-born of all creation
18b	the first-born from the dead
16a	for in him were created all things
19ab	for in him was pleased all the fullness to dwell
16b	in heaven and on earth
20c	whether things on earth or things in heaven
16e	all things through him and unto him were created
20a	and through him to reconcile all things unto him
17a	and he is before all things
18a	and he is the head of the body

It is also helpful to place the similar material in parallel columns:

Who is the image of the invisible God	Who is the beginning
the first-born of all creation	the first-born of the dead
for in him were created all things	for in him was pleased all the fullness to dwell
in heaven and on earth	and through him to reconcile all things unto him
all things through him and unto him were created.	whether things on earth or things in heaven.

But the hymn contains other literary devices. In the two clauses beginning with "for in him" (1:16 and 19–20a) the three preposi- tions "in," "through," and "unto" occur and in the same sequence.

Chiasmus, which is parallelism in reverse order (ab - ba), is found in 1:16d and 1:20a, 1:16a and e, 1:16b and c, and 1:16b and 20c.

| 16d | a all things | b through him and |
| 20a | b and through him | a all things |

Inclusio, which is surrounding or forming a circle around a group of words with the same word or same group of words, is found in 1:16a to e through the repetition of "all things . . . were created." The piling up of statements with the word "all" is another literary device found in both Greek and Jewish hymnody. In this case within six verses seven statements are made with "all." The piling up of the third person singular pronoun "he" adds to this literary device.

The complex matrix of literary devices demonstrates that 1:15–20 is a poem, a hymn. Did the author of the letter compose it himself or did he find it being used by the churches in southern Asia Minor? The fact that the hymn begins with "who" indicates that only part of the hymn is being quoted. Elsewhere in the NT relative clauses also begin the quotation of a hymn (Phil. 2:6, 1 Tim. 3:16; Heb. 1:3; 1 Pet. 2:22). But other stylistic indications that the author quoted or modified the hymn are more difficult to establish for the simple reason that absolute regularity cannot be presupposed in the original. And the author of the letter may have skillfully modified the hymn. On the other hand, those elements of the hymn which are regular are probably original. For the rest it is necessary to use content as well as form to try to determine what changes may have been made.

In 1:18a "of the church" has been added. Not only has it been done in the author's own style of loosely adding on explanations, but the context shows that the "body" at this point means the whole cosmos. By these words "of the church" the author applies the cosmic hymn to the congregation in Colossae (cf. 1:24; 2:19).

In 1:20b "through the blood of his cross" has been added.

"Making peace" occurs only here in the NT, and thus does not reflect Pauline terminology. "Through him" by itself probably would not have been added, so that the awkward reduplication of "through" comes from the author of the letter. The hymn by itself in 1:18bc and 19–20a has affirmed that in Christ because of his resurrection and because of the fullness dwelling in him, the cosmos has been reconciled. Just as the author added the "church," so he added the reference to the "cross" (cf. 2:14) in order to tie reconciliation to the forgiveness of sins (1:14) through the historical event of the cross. To be sure, the parallel in Heb. 1:3 has both the cosmic dimension and the historical event of the atonement (if it is not redactional), but the re-duplicated "through," the author's style of loosely adding on explanations, and the typical Pauline addition of the cross (cf. Phil. 2:8) militate against this phrase being part of the original hymn.

It is not possible to be as definite about other possible additions. In 1:16cd there is the list: "visible and invisible, whether thrones or dominions or principalities or powers." The first two terms in the list sum up the whole cosmos according to Hellenistic terminology, but all the "powers" are invisible according to Jewish thinking, and this is a clue to another addition by the author of the letter. He added the final four from a typical Jewish listing to make his point that the "principalities and powers" which were important to his opponents are subject to Christ, who is the "head" (1:18; 2:10), the "beginning" (1:18), and the conqueror (2:15) of all the powers.

In 1:18d stands the clause: "in order that he may be preeminent in all things." There is no parallel clause in 1:15, and this final clause does not logically fit with the causal clause which follows in 1:19. The subjunctive "might be" could be a note of incompleteness which conflicts with the stress on completeness in the rest of the hymn. However, the verb "to be preeminent" occurs only here in the NT, which may mean that it is original.

Finally, in 1:20c there is the concluding line: "whether things on earth or things in heaven." It is parallel to 1:16b and simply repeats the "all" theme once again. Another "through him" without the concluding line would be awkward. Yet it is also similar to the "whether . . . or" addition in 1:16d, and may again have been an attempt by the author of the letter to stress the totality of Christ's rule. The quotation of the hymn did not begin with the beginning and may not have concluded with the conclusion.

The hymn was used by the churches in southern Asia Minor. The first stanza stresses creation and the second redemption. The "image of the invisible God" (1:15) does not mean simply the "reflection" of God, for Hellenistic terminology requires that in an "image" what is represented is present (Wisdom is the "image" of God. Wis. Sol. 7:25–26). Since Christ represents the "invisible God," he is not part of creation, but God's revelation and God's instrument. Thus something else is meant here than in 3:10, where the new man is to be renewed after the image of the creator. As the context demonstrates in 1:15–16 and in 1:18bc, "the first-born of all creation" does not mean in Arian fashion that Christ is part of creation, even though he is the first-born. In Hellenistic Wisdom speculation the same kind of terminology was used to describe Wisdom as the one who was created "at the beginning" and "before all things" (Prov. 8:22; Sir. 1:4; 24:9). In similar terms the hymn depicts Christ's superiority over the whole cosmos.

The next verse spells out the implications of 1:15. He is God's instrument of creation for the totality of the cosmos, both at the beginning, indicated by the aorist tense in the first verb, and also now, indicated by the perfect tense in the second verb. The three prepositions "in," "through," and "unto" with "all" are similar to Stoic and then Hellenistic-Jewish statements about God and the cosmos. Christ is the sphere in whom the world was created, he is the instrument through whom the world is created, and he is the eschatological goal unto whom the world is created. The eschatological note points forward to the soteriological emphasis in the second stanza. V. 17 repeats what was said in 1:15 about Christ's priority ("before all things") and in 1:16 about Christ's sustaining work as creator ("have held together"—perfect tense). In 1:18a a parallel sentence to 1:17 designates Christ as the head, the sovereign, of the body. The context demonstrates that separation instead of similarity is meant. "The body" is a typical Hellenistic image for the whole cosmos, and this "cosmos" is understood to have a "head." In the undisputed Pauline letters Christ is never called the head of the body.

The second stanza starts by affirming that Christ is "the beginning." (In Hellenistic Judaism Wisdom is "at the beginning," Prov. 8:22.) To be the "beginning" is to be the "first-born from the dead," the resurrected one. But Christ is more than the first-born as the one who has a temporal priority, although he is that also (Rom. 8:29; Rev. 1:5). The context demonstrates that Christ in his resurrection sums up everything that must be said against death; he is the sphere in whom life is as it is in the creator. V. 19 expands on what is implied in 18bc: "for all the fullness," meaning all the fullness of God, God himself, was pleased to dwell in Christ. The Hellenistic concept of "fullness" is used to express how in Christ "all" of God was present. The aorist infinitive "to dwell" along with "was pleased" may refer to a specific time when God elected to dwell in Christ, but nothing in the hymn makes it possible to determine which time. Finally in 1:20 the aorist infinitive "to reconcile," which is parallel to "to dwell" in 1:19, points to the fact that in Christ the whole cosmos has already been reconciled. (The word used here for "reconcile" is not a Pauline term.) The familiar triad of prepositions (cf. 1:16) "in," "through," and "unto" (1:19–20) stresses that Christ is the sphere, the instrument, and the eschatological goal of this reconciliation. The aorist participle "having made peace" simply repeats the theme, that all things on earth and heaven have already been reconciled through Christ.

The author of the letter to the Colossians interpreted the hymn by additions and by the verses which follow. He added 1:16cd, 18d, and perhaps 20c in order to underline the completeness of Christ's primacy. More importantly, he added "of the church" to 1:18a and "through the blood of his cross" to 1:20b in order to bring the cosmic eschatology of the hymn back into the realm of history. To be sure, a kind of cosmic history is implied by the triad of prepositions. The "powers" not only exist in a kind of timeless state of having been reconciled to Christ, but they are also subject to Christ, the head of the cosmos, so that some dramatic tension is present. Nevertheless, the author of the letter corrected the non-historical tendency of the hymn. While Christ remains Lord of the cosmos, he rules it through his only body, the church. "Reconciliation" has taken place in Christ precisely because of the "blood of the cross" and not because of any cosmic drama. Even the reference to the resurrection in the "first-born from the dead" could by itself be understood in too cosmic, too syncretistic a fashion. What the author of the letter added may seem patchy in places, but it must be understood as his attempt to keep the hymn within the Pauline branch of Christianity.

THE ESCHATOLOGY OF THE LETTER
TO THE COLOSSIANS

Was the original hymn Christian? Yes, because "first-born from the dead" could only come from a Christian context. But was not the original hymn Pauline? Similarities do exist between the hymn and Pauline terminology. The fragment of a creed in 1 Cor. 8:6 places Christ on an equality with God and declares that all things exist "through" him. In Rom. 11:36 all things are "from," "through," and "unto" God. Christ is the "first-born" (Rom. 8:29), the "wisdom" of God (1 Cor. 1:24, 30), and the "image" of God (2 Cor. 4:4). Paul writes of "powers" of various kinds; some are subject to Christ (1 Cor. 2:8; Phil. 2:10, although this may be cited from a hymn).

However, the issue is not one of terminology, but theology. The issue is whether Paul's theology includes both static, two-level thinking and dynamic, forward-looking thinking.

In the letter to the Colossians there is no question but that there are two levels, the world above and the world below. In 1:5 hope is "laid up for you in heaven." In 3:1: "seek the things that are above, where Christ is." This kind of spatial thinking was common in Qumran and in contemporary Judaism.

Paul too can write of final salvation in spatial terms: we shall be caught up "in the clouds to meet the Lord in the air" (1 Thess. 4:17; cf. 1:10; Phil. 3:20), but it must be admitted that most of the time Paul uses temporal-eschatological descriptions of final salvation. Throughout his writings Paul uses the future tense in statements about Christians being included with Christ in his resurrection (Rom. 6:8; 1 Cor. 15:22; 2 Cor. 4:14; 13:4; Phil. 3:10–11).

On the other hand, in the letter to the Colossians the present and completed nature of salvation is stressed throughout. "He has delivered us," "we have redemption" (1:13–14). "You were raised with him through faith" (2:12; 3:1). You "have put on" the new (3:10). As the hymn to Christ puts it, "all things" have been reconciled "in" and "unto" Christ (1:19–20). Salvation is a fact; what happens now and in the future is that it is made known and made manifest. "The mystery hidden for ages" is "now made manifest" (1:26; cf. 1:5; 1:27; but also Paul, Rom. 8:24; 1 Cor. 2:7, 10). "You were raised with Christ" (3:1); now this is hidden, but when he appears, "then you also will appear with him in glory" (3:3–4; but cf. Paul, Phil. 3:20). The future is used only in terms of rewards and punishments for the works one has done (3:6, 24; also Paul, Rom. 2:6; 1 Cor. 3:13–15; 2 Cor. 5:10; 9:6; Gal. 6:7–9).

How different then is the letter to the Colossians from Paul? Is all of this a distinction with no real difference? To claim that the letter to the Colossians is "Gnostic" is too simple. The opponents insisted on certain requirements which still must be fulfilled. Yet a certain tendency toward realized eschatology cannot be denied. There is no trace of an imminent parousia. Nor can it be claimed that a spatial rather than a temporal approach is just a different mind-set but the meaning is the same. The images of growth, to be sure, do point to a kind of eschatological tension (1:6, 10; 2:7, 19), as do perhaps even the exhortations throughout the letter, but it is not the same tension as in Paul, for whom resurrection with Christ is something radically new, something in the future.

Nevertheless, is not the difference to be explained by the fact that Paul adapted himself to the needs of the situation, becoming "all things to all men" (1 Cor. 9:22)? According to this argument, the opponents insisted on certain requirements; instead of hope, they proclaimed uncertainty. In this polemic situation, Paul's theology shifted in order to affirm the certainty of salvation and freedom from all requirements, without, of course, proclaiming license, as is proven by his exhortations.

However, what is involved is not merely similarities or differences in terminology (although terms must be examined) or a slight adaptation in theology, which surely Paul often did. What is involved is the fact that the total shape of the theology is different. For example, in Paul the motivation for the Christian life is the future resurrection with Christ, whereas in this letter the motivation is baptism. The change in perspective is present not only in the patently polemic sections of the letter, but all through it.

The eschatology of the original hymn merits separate attention. How can a cosmos which was created in, through, and unto Christ and which is held together in Christ be in further need of reconciliation? It has been reconciled. As a consequence the hymn has been the basic proof-text for those holding the doctrine of universal salvation, *apokatastasis*. The strength of this position is that it can point to the repeated use of "all" and the use of present and aorist tenses. Therefore, according to those holding this doctrine, as for example Sittler at New Delhi in 1961, in the "cosmic Christ" all things, both man and nature, have been and are reconciled. Those who hold to a "Christology of nature" such as that associated with the name of Teilhard de Chardin also took to this text for support.

The radical implications of this "triumphalistic" position for ethics and for the mission of the church are self-evident. Criticisms have not been lacking. For example, according to the hymn reconciliation has already been accomplished, while in the apocalyptic fragment in Rom. 8:19–23 the whole creation will be freed only in the future. In Rom. 8:20 the "creation was subjected to futility, not of its own will," but God's, while in Col. 1:15–20, although the hymn does not indicate that the cosmos has fallen, it had to be "reconciled." Even the consideration that man is part of creation and included the cosmos in his fall does not clear up the difficulty.

But more than exegetical detail is at stake, for two basic methodological questions lurk in the background. First, how does one move from history or a historical text to doctrine, and second, what is the relationship between the original hymn and the canon? As far as the first question is concerned, 1:15–20 is a hymn, not a series of doctrinal propositions. It was used in the worship of the early church, but it is impossible to specify exactly where, since sacramental imagery in 1:12–14 does not belong to the original context of the hymn and nothing in the hymn itself indicates where it was used. In any case, the hymn was doxological. It focused totally on Christ as the only Lord and Savior, not on the nature of the cosmos or its inhabitants. The hymn did not intend or imply a theology (Christology) of nature, and only an over-reading of the text will find a theology of nature in it. As far as the second question, the canon, is concerned, the reconstructed original hymn is and always will remain disputed. Whatever is agreed upon about the original will throw light on 1:15–20, of course, but in order to avoid the ravages of exegetical subjectivity, the canonical text remains the basis for preaching and teaching. This maxim is not a way of avoiding difficulties, including subjective difficulties, which must always be faced while interpreting the text, but of avoiding the greater danger.

The Application of the Hymn

"And you" (1:21) begins the application of the hymn to the church at Colossae. Elements of the hymn reappear in "reconcile" (1:20 and 22), "through death" (1:20 and 22), and the cosmic dimension (1:16 and 23). "Then" contrasted with "but now" (1:21–22; also 1:26b; 3:7–8) is terminology well-known in early Christian preaching. The reconciliation of the whole cosmos found in the hymn is applied with cultic and legal terminology (1:22) to the historical reconciliation of Christians "before" Christ. Reconciliation, however, must produce lives that show the effects of Christ's rule (1:22–23). To "continue in the faith" and not shift "from the hope . . . which you heard" is the same static, objectifying tendency seen earlier in this chapter (1:5–7, 9). The cosmic terminology of the hymn reappears with "the whole creation" (1:23), but interpreted historically as the mission to "all people." The emphatic "I" brings out the fact that only Paul is the minister of the gospel to "all people." "Minister of the gospel" is not an expression found in the generally accepted letters of Paul.

The last clause, about Paul's ministry, leads directly to the next section. The much-disputed verse 1:24 becomes far less difficult when the context is kept in mind. The author does not suddenly abandon his position that salvation has been completed in Christ. (Cf. also 2:13–14.) Nor is there any stress on substitutionary atonement through these sufferings and tribulations, although the traditional interpretation of this verse as portraying a mystic union between Christ's passion and Paul holds that the sufferings are substitutionary. To hold this interpretation, of course, cannot help but give even more importance to the unique office of Paul than the previous verse. However, the key to this passage is its apocalyptic background, according to which God has predestined a certain quantity of suffering before the end can come. (Cf. 1 Enoch 47:4; Rev. 6:11; Mark 13:19–20 par.) Apocalyptic terms color this whole section, even though the apocalyptic expectation of the imminent end is not found in the letter to the Colossians: "tribulations" (1:24), "the mystery hidden . . . but now made manifest" (1:26: cf. 1 Enoch 10:7), "the riches of the glory of this mystery" (1:27: cf. Rev. 5:12), "God's mystery" (2:2).

The first half of 1:24 is parallel with the second; "for your sake" includes more than the church at Colossae, and is equivalent to "for the sake of his body," which as in the hymn (1:18) is interpreted to be the church. What is "lacking" is not something in the Colossians or the church, for Christ "has reconciled" them (1:22). The intention of 1:24 is, like that of 1:23 and 1:25, to bring out the authority of Paul's unique office. He alone is the minister of the gospel to all people (1:23), he is the minister of the church "according to the divine office given to me for you" in order to "complete the word of God" (1:25; cf. 1:23 and Rom. 15:19), and his unique office includes the sufferings by which he completes "what is lacking . . . for your sake" (1:24). His sufferings belong to his unique office for the sake of the church. They are an integral part of God's plan and thus are part of Paul's apostolic authority. Paul had often written of how the Christian shares in Christ's sufferings (Rom. 8:17, 35–36; 2 Cor. 1:3–7; Phil. 1:29–30; 3:10). In 1 Cor. 4:9–13 and 2 Cor. 4:10–12 a kind of suffering for the sake of others is indicated, but there is a great possibility that Paul is being ironic about those in Corinth who imagine they are strong. He does, however, describe his own sufferings (and tribulations) as part of his apostolic ministry (2 Cor. 4:5; 6:3–10; 11:22–33; 12:9–10; 13:4; 1 Thess. 3:3–4; cf. Rom. 9:3). In later NT writings Paul is said to suffer for the sake of others (Eph. 3:1, 13; 2 Tim. 2:10; cf. Acts 9:16). Col. 1:24 may be a step in this later direction. What is distinctive about 1:24 is that Paul's sufferings are said to be unique, obviously put this way because of the emphasis in this section on his apostolic authority.

In 1:25–29 how the gospel comes to the world through Paul's unique ministry continues to be spelled out. The Colossians are mentioned personally, but they really stand for the church universal ("you" in 1:23–25, 27). Using a well-known early Christian formula, "once salvation was hidden, but now it has been manifested" (1 Cor. 2:7–10; 2 Tim. 1:9–10), the author brings out the fact that the mystery, "Christ in you," was hidden from others but is now made known in the church, which includes "all people" (1:23), the gentiles. The same objectifying tendency found in 1:5–7, 9 and 23 appears again in "to make known . . . the hope" and "teaching" (1:27–28). "Teaching" in association with "admonish" and "wisdom" (cf. 3:16) is, to be sure, a very practical matter (cf. 1:9–10). The purpose of this apostolic effort is also practical, that every man be "mature in Christ" (cf. 1:22; 4:12). And in a very specific fashion Paul himself, because Christ works in him (1:29), strives toward this goal. "We" in 1:28 indicates that others with Paul proclaim Christ. The return to "I" in 1:29 is part of the transition to Paul's specific concern for the Colossians in 2:1, as is the repetition of the similar-sounding Greek words for "striving."

By means of 2:1–5 the author establishes Paul's presence even though he is absent. He is present "in spirit" (2:5), which does not here mean in the "Holy Spirit," but in "himself," "in his thoughts." As in the hymn to Christ, redundancy and the repetition of "all" are used to emphasize Christ's uniqueness ("all the riches of the fullness," "all the treasures," 2:2–3; cf. 3:11). For

the first time trouble in the church at Colossae is mentioned openly
(2:4), and this provides the opportunity once again to bring out
the settled and objective nature of their faith ("knowledge," 2:2;
"wisdom and knowledge," 2:3; "firmness of your faith," 2:5; cf.
"established in the faith just as you were taught," 2:7).

THE UNDERSTANDING OF THE CHURCH IN
THE LETTER TO THE COLOSSIANS

To what degree is the understanding of the church in this letter
Pauline? Paul had written about the church as the "body of
Christ" (Rom. 12:4–5; 1 Cor. 6:12–20; 10:17; 12:12–27), but
never that Christ is the head of the body. Over against the
opponents, who did not "hold fast to the Head" (2:19) but to
"principalities and powers" (2:10, 15) the author of the letter to
the Colossians insisted that Christ is the head of every principality
and power. In the original hymn Christ is the head of the body,
the cosmos (1:18), and thus the hymn provided a kind of proof-
text. However, the author modified the hymn by limiting Christ's
body to the church (1:18, 24; cf. 3:15), and as a consequence
Christ was described as the head of the church. This is clearly a
step beyond Paul's usage, yet it is possible that, because of the
polemic situation, Paul developed the image of the "body of
Christ" in this direction himself.

Another indication that the letter to the Colossians was close
to Paul is the fact that except for serving as "minister" (1:7, 23,
25; 4:7), the author mentions no church office or structure. In
fact, church members are to "teach and admonish one another"
(3:16). Nevertheless, there are differences. Paul never uses
"minister of the gospel" or "minister of the church" (1:23, 25),
but this is an argument from silence and therefore weak. Paul is
the only apostle mentioned, but this is again to argue from silence.
A strong argument is the emphatic "I, Paul" in 1:23 and the
reasoning in the following verses. "I, Paul" along with the clause
in which it stands is hardly an incidental transition to the next
section. Three emphatic statements are grouped together: "I,
Paul" am a "minister," "I complete what is lacking," and I am a
"minister . . . to complete the word," to reveal Christ to all people.

Thus Paul not only had an unshared, unrepeatable function, but this function is part of the unique action in which salvation came. Paul did at times speak very highly of his function, yet this is something more, for example, than Rom. 2:16 and Gal. 1:15–16 and different from the personal emphasis which is found in Paul's ethical exhortations (1 Cor. 11:1; 2 Cor. 10:1; Gal. 5:2; Phil. 4:9). As the author of the letter to the Colossians developed his argument, he brought out Paul's unique position in order to give authority to Paul's message. His message, of course, has implications for the Christian life, but these practical implications develop out of the message guaranteed by the unique position Paul holds. At this point, even though the polemic situation can be used to explain many differences between the letter to the Colossians and the Pauline writings, a step has been taken beyond Paul.

POLEMIC APPLICATION OF THE LORDSHIP
OF CHRIST TO THE SITUATION IN COLOSSAE

Col. 2:6–7 is a thematic summary, similar to 3:1–4, which looks, Janus-like, both to the basis of their faith and to its application to the Christian life, and provides, as a consequence, a kind of conclusion as well as transition. The rest of the chapter then brings the conflict with the opponents into the open.

First, using the theme of the hymn, Christ is Lord of all, the author carried on a debate with the opponents' "philosophy" (2:8–15). "Ensnare" (2:8) has an evil connotation. "Philosophy" does not mean an intellectual discipline, but rather philosophical teachings with a religious orientation. "Empty deceit" is a harsh judgment on the opponents. "Christ" stands in contrast with "human tradition" and the "elements." The next two verses are a polemic exegesis of the hymn (1:16, 18–19). The intent of these and the following verses is to bring out the fact that in Christ salvation is already full and complete. "In" or "with" Christ is repeated throughout the section (2:9–15) in order to draw it together around this motif. The author makes frequent use of traditional phrases and images. A lack of divine "fullness" in Christ (2:9) is obviously one of the claims of the opponents. "Bodily" in this context means "really" and perhaps Christ's body. Christians have already reached "fullness" in him; the opponents possibly held that faith in Christ is not enough. Circumcision (2:11) means baptism and that it was "made without hands" refers to the fact that God has done it. Since 2:11-12 probably develops Rom. 6:4-6 or a common source, "body of flesh" (Rom. 6:6) is the same as "body of sin." The "circumcision of Christ" is the circumcision which Christ gives, that is, baptism. Rom. 6:4 lies behind "buried with him" in 2:12, but in characteristic fashion the author interprets Paul by adding "raised with him through faith." Could 2:13-15 be another hymnic fragment? Probably not. Extensive parallelism and dramatic imagery create a kind of poetic atmosphere, but both style and theology are too close to that of the author of the letter. In 2:13 the shift from second to first person plural is explained by the sense of the verse; Paul could not be included among the uncircumcised, but did belong with all those whom "God made alive" in Christ. The main point of these verses is clear and should not be lost in the profusion of what are to some extent mixed metaphors. Unusual words may reflect the opponents' terminology. In 2:13-15 God is the one who is acting. "All" trespasses have been forgiven. He "wiped away" or cancelled the "IOU against us" with its "regulations" (2:14a). Schweizer points out that the same word for "regulations" is used in Pythagorean philosophy. "Why do you submit to regulations?" (2:20) is a verb with the same root. The "regulations," as for example in 2:16 and 21, are requirements the opponents claim are necessary for salvation. "What was against us, even that he removed, nailing it to the cross" (2:14b). The point is clear, the picture jumbled. Both that Christ bore our sins and that the accusation against the crucified person was posted on his cross may be intended. God disarmed the principalities and powers. (Cf. 1:16; 2:10.) He exhibited them as spoils of war, the way a conqueror does, triumphing over them in Christ. (Cf. 2 Cor. 2:14.) The parallel of Col. 2:15 with 2:14 could mean that "in the cross" should be used instead of "in Christ" at this point; it would not change the sense.

Second, the author applied the theme, Christ is Lord of all, to the concrete teachings of the opponents, which were, as was noted in the opening section, somewhat syncretistic. Although the word "freedom" is not used, it is in fact what the author brings out. The argument is made up of two antitheses (2:16–17 and 18–19) and a dilemma (2:20–23). In the first antithesis the regulations are not fully contrasted with Christ, however, for "shadow" is compared with "body," reality, but the provisional nature of "shadows" comes out in the flow of the argument. "Body" keeps the focus on the church. In the second antithesis cultic require- ments are mocked (cf. "empty deceit" 2:8); the opponents want to cheat you out of the prize of salvation by insisting on ritual humil- ity, the worship of angels, and visions, but this is to be puffed up in vain by the fleshly mind, the mind which is not full of Christ. They are not holding fast to the head, Christ (the metaphor can- not be pressed). He is head (cf. 1:18; 2:10) of the whole body (cf. 2:17), and thus cares for every need. The final three verses set up a dilemma which appeals not only to Christ but also, with a touch of irony, to common sense. The "if" clause sums up what has been proven in order to establish one horn of the dilemma. On this basis the author could ask embarrassing questions about "regulations," "human commandments and doctrines." Common sense also knows these things all perish and that what seem to be wise ascetic practices have no value, except for indulging the flesh.

THE ETHICAL APPLICATION:
LIVE WHAT YOU ARE IN CHRIST

A thematic summary (3:1–4; cf. 2:6–7) which is both a con- clusion and a transition focuses the issue: since you are free from the "regulations" because Christ is Lord of all and you have died and been raised with him, live in him. The first two verses echo 2:12–13. The second pair of verses is written in progressive parallelism. Since the new life is still hidden (3:3–4), it is neces- sary to point out what it should be.

Another pivotal "therefore" begins the section which applies the thematic summary first negatively (3:5–11), then positively (12–17). These two sections are very similar, almost parallel, in the way the argument is developed. The first section is again divided in two parts, according to the two lists of five vices, and these two parts are connected by the formula "then . . . but now" (3:7–8a; cf. 1:21–22); vv. 7a and 8a are also in chiastic parallelism. Lists of vices and virtues each totalling five were very traditional, and for the Pythagoreans five was the key number. For the author of the letter to the Colossians these lists became building blocks for his argument, the contrast between the old and the new which has been initiated by baptism. (Cf. 1:12, 21–22; 2:13.) A secondary contrast is between the first list of vices, which are those of the gentiles and which in traditional fashion are described as leading to the final judgment, and the second list of vices, which are especially those endangering communal life among Christians. Since these are traditional lists, specific references to the situation at Colossae cannot be supposed. "Earthly members" (3:5) does not refer to parts of the body, but is a metaphor for vices, as the context demonstrates. The metaphor "put away" (cf. Rom. 13:12) is switched in the following verses to "put off . . . put on" (3:8–10; cf. Rom. 13:12–14). There are no pre-Christian parallels to the metaphor of "putting off the old man" and "putting on the new." The metaphor must not be pressed, for one cannot put off himself, except of course in the sense of dying and rising with Christ in baptism. (Cf. 2:11–12; Gal. 3:27.) The present imperative "do not lie" governs these two aorist participles; thus they describe the entrance into a condition, baptism, which is to be carried out. The Christian "is being renewed," a continuing, daily process, in knowledge, according to the image (Christ's) of his (the Christian's) creator (God). The old man did not have the image of God; he is not "being renewed." But the new man, new precisely because he has been baptized into Christ, who alone is truly the image of God (1:15), has the task of reflecting this image "in knowledge," which is not theoretical, but practical. (Cf. 1:9–10.) The practical consequence is seen in the fact that every conflict between opposing factions has already been overcome (3:11; cf. 1 Cor. 12:13; Gal. 3:28), for Christ is already all and in all. The author concludes with his familiar emphasis on "all." "Scythian" refers to a group thought to be very barbarous, and therefore "barbarian, Scythian" is not a complete antithesis.

The second section (3:12–17) once again uses "therefore," the image of "putting on," and a traditional list, this time of five virtues. "Elect," "holy," and "beloved" remind the Colossians of the basis on which they stand. The five virtues, and "love" (3:14), "peace" (3:15), "thankfulness" (3:15, 17), and "wisdom" (3:16) all describe practical actions, not abstract attitudes. The present tense in "forbearing" and "forgiving" indicates that continuing action is expected. The "Lord" is the risen Christ, and what he has done is the impelling basis for the Christian life. "Love" (cf. Rom. 13:8, 10; 1 Corinthians 13) binds everything together and produces perfection, which is not, however, abstract sinlessness, but, as the context shows, living by forgiveness. The "peace of Christ" is a power which creates the "one body," the church. "Thanksgiving" is a frequent theme in this letter (1:3, 12; 2:7; 3:15, 17; 4:2), and the following verse describes how to give thanks. It is to let the living "Word," Christ, dwell "in you" (cf. 1:27); and this will create a specific kind of life and worship. "Psalms and hymns and songs" are very difficult to distinguish from one another. "In the grace" can be understood as "graciously" and "with thanks," but the absolute meaning of God's "grace" (cf. 4:18) must be kept to the fore because of the definite article "the." In a concluding verse which both sums up this part and provides the theological basis for the following section, the author once again has centered all of the Christian life in Christ. (Cf. 3:11; Rom. 14:23c.)

CONCRETE APPLICATION TO LIFE
IN THE HOUSEHOLD

It might be claimed that 3:18–4:1 was inserted here in the letter, for, if the section had been removed, it would be impossible to discern the omission. This helps to demonstrate the separateness and unity of what is commonly called the Colossian *Haustafel* or social code. The ancient world had, of course, developed various ideas about right and wrong, what might be described as conventional morality about social relationships. In time especially the Stoics and later Hellenistic Judaism gave more shape to this material by developing traditional "rules for social relationships."

The oldest and simplest Christian social code is found in the letter to the Colossians. (Cf. for later codes: Eph. 5:22–6:9; 1 Pet. 2:13–3:7; Tit. 2:1–10; 1 Clem. 21:6–9; Ign. Pol. 4:1–6:1; Did. 4:9–11; Pol. Phil. 4:1–6:3; Barn. 19:5–7.) It shows indications of this background by its use of traditional Hellenistic moral terminology: "as is fitting" (3:18), "pleasing" (3:20), and "justly and fairly" (4:1), by its stress on "being subject," and by its arrangement of social relationships according to pairs.

The Colossian social code starts with the most intimate family tie and moves toward the more distant relationships. Each pair of relationships begins with the subordinate member. Each group is addressed with the direct article plus the nominative case, an imperative, and then its basis. This intricate structure, the traditional materials, and the fact that a normal transition, such as "therefore," is missing in 3:18, all indicate that specific concerns at Colossae are not being addressed. Nevertheless there are two possible reasons for this material at this point. First, in 3:11 Christian freedom from many social distinctions had been described, although the equality of "male and female" found in Gal. 3:28 does not appear. Freedom for women and slaves could begin to be very disruptive to the social fabric, and the author would have inserted this material as a corrective. To be sure, all the groups are admonished, not simply the subordinate ones, but that was part of the tradition. "Children" are not potential revolutionaries but they are included because Hellenistic Judaism grouped together those three pairs of relationships which make up the totality of the household. Second, the author, by centering Christian life "in the Lord," was fighting against ascetic "regulations" pushed by his opponents.

Traditional materials were adapted for Christian use. First of all, they are modified by the context, which is "seeking that which is above because you have been raised with Christ" (3:1), and "forgiving," "love," "peace," and worship (3:13–16). Second, the final judgment is brought in (3:24–25; cf. 3:6). Third, "in the Lord," "the Lord Christ," or simply the "Lord" (cf. 1:10) is added, at times like a formula (3:20). Fourth, the weaker groups are given more protection than was usual in contemporary ethics.

All in all, the author's intent is to describe how living in Christ does not mean escape from this world, but instead concrete involvement in the daily realities of this world. However, the concrete rules and realities of this world do not have the last word, for they are continually challenged by the Lordship of Christ, who transforms all of life (3:11, 17).

"Wives" are to be "subject" (3:18). According to the understanding of social relationships at that time, this is what is "fitting," and thus in no way was it understood as demeaning. But the basis is changed radically; it "is fitting in the Lord." Husbands, for their part, are to "love," which is also a radical departure from traditional commands in this context. "Love" in 2:2 and 3:14 helps us understand the meaning here. "Do not be embittered" spells out one implication of this love. "Children" are to obey because it is "pleasing," again normal reasoning at that time, but then "in the Lord" transforms that normal reasoning. "Fathers," parents, including mothers (cf. 3:20), are to show love to their children by not, among other things, provoking them. The basis, to be sure, is simply good secular common sense: "lest they become discouraged." The longer section on "slaves" and "masters" (3:22–4:1) may be a sign that slavery had become an issue for the church. "Slaves" are to obey "in all things," and what this means is elaborated on in the remainder of 3:22; v. 23 is parallel to v. 22. The basis is the final judgment (3:24–25), and "fearing the Lord" (3:22–24), which in this context means "having respect for what Christ commands." "Serve" (3:24) is an imperative like "obey" and "work" (3:22–23). "Masters" have already been put in their place by being called "according to the flesh" (3:22), but they are also to be limited by "justness" and "fairness," well-known concepts in contemporary morality. Again, the fact that masters have a master in heaven transforms these concepts.

The author concluded the ethical application of the theme: "live what you are in Christ," with traditional directives about prayer and evangelism (4:2–6). "Being watchful" (4:2) and "redeeming the time" (4:5) are not a warning of the last judgment, but describe the general readiness of the Christian to use opportunities as they come. Paul is to "make manifest" (cf. 3:4) the word, the mystery of Christ (cf. 1:27; 2:2), but God alone opens doors. The last two verses give directions about mission work. That their speech should "always be gracious, seasoned with salt" is probably a standard turn of phrase.

THE CONCLUSION OF THE LETTER

The conclusion begins with recommendations for Tychicus and Onesimus. The list of greetings is unusually long. (Cf., however, Rom. 16:3-16, 21-23.) Every name in the letter to Philemon except Philemon and Apphia appears in the conclusion to the letter to the Colossians. "Minister" (4:7) and "ministry" (4:17) refer to performing a service, not to an office. Paul underscores the important role held by Epaphras, as he had done earlier in the letter (4:12-13; cf. 1:7-8). "That you may stand perfect and be filled with all the will of God" picks up again, as in 2:2, the opponents' stress on "fullness." That they should exchange letters with Laodicea (4:16) may indicate how Paul's letters were circulated and gradually collected. It was customary to conclude a dictated letter with a personally written greeting. The benediction does not appear to be Pauline because it is shorter than all the Pauline benedictions except for the Pastorals.

THE AUTHOR OF THE LETTER
TO THE COLOSSIANS

The different vocabulary and style of the letter to the Colossians have often been used to prove that Paul did not write this letter. Such claims may seem to belong in the same category with claims that Bacon wrote Shakespeare. The mistake of approaching the differences in vocabulary simply in terms of statistics, particularly when used to argue from silence, is evident. However, just as each person has distinctive fingerprints and even a "voice-print" which cannot be imitated by someone else, so each person has a "language-print." Bujard has been able to demonstrate, by examining the complete "print" of the style and vocabulary in the letter to the Colossians and comparing it with the equivalent in Paul, that Paul could not have written the letter to the Colossians. It is a matter of such things as the subconscious turn of a phrase, the use of particles, connectives, and prepositions in a particular fashion, and the habitual shape of the sentence. The letter to the Colossians is permeated with a definite style. The difference between it and Paul's style is greater than can be accounted for by adjustments in style and vocabulary because of old age, living in prison, using the opponents' terminology, the occasional use of a liturgical or hymnic style, or the polemic setting.

On the other hand, the personal references in the conclusion (4:7–18) are almost identical with those in Philemon, but not in the same sequence. In one case Epaphras is the fellow-prisoner (Philem. 23), in the other Aristarchus (4:10). This does not seem to indicate simple imitation, and in this letter it is hard to imagine the motive for such extensive fabrication. To be sure, there is the example of the Pastoral letters, which were written in order to establish several of Paul's followers as his legitimate successors; however, this does not seem to be the motive behind the letter to the Colossians. To the pseudonymous author fabrication was not falsification, but an accepted method of carrying on the genuine tradition as long as one of its apostolic guarantors continued to be a living memory within the author's milieu.

Secretaries and editors have been the usual way of explaining difficulties and differences. There were editors and Paul did dictate, but the issue is: what did Paul himself write? If what exists at present is the result of editing or of Paul's giving his secretaries the general idea of what he wanted to say and letting them compose his letters, then Paul is only indirectly the author. However, since the theology of this letter goes beyond Paul, it is better not to think of secretaries, but of a Pauline school which was developing already during Paul's life. This would explain both the close association of this letter with the letter to Philemon and the intermediate theological position which the letter to the Colossians has between Paul and later pseudonymous writings. This intermediate position was close to Paul in that it kept to his emphasis on Christ's Lordship, baptism, freedom from the "elements" and "regulations," and living out one's faith in ordinary existence; but it had begun to draw away from Paul in 1) the way its eschatology was shaped, for example, that the motivation for ethics was baptism instead of being raised with Christ at the parousia, 2) its concern for the authority of Paul's unique position, 3) its stress on knowledge, wisdom, correct teaching, and "making manifest" even though the practical side of these concepts is not forgotten, and, on the other hand, 4) the absence of central Pauline concepts such as the Holy Spirit (in 1:8–9; 3:16 "spiritually" simply contrasts with "worldly"), the law, and justification, which would have been astonishing for Paul because the opponents were not "enthusiasts" at all, but were surely "legalists." Speculation about a possible author has hit upon Timothy, Philemon, or Epaphras, but it is impossible to do more than speculate.

When was the letter to the Colossians written? Colossae was probably destroyed by an earthquake in A.D. 61 or 62, but coins have been found showing that a town existed at Colossae until at least the third century A.D. According to the letter to the Colossians, Paul had not visited Colossae (1:4, 7–9; 2:1; cf. Acts 16:6; 18:23). It is probable that Epaphras founded the church (1:7–8; 4:12–13). Paul is described as being in prison, although the place is not identified (1:24; 4:3, 10, 18). However, the letter is pseudonymous, and the time and place of its composition can only be inferred. Its theology shows that members of Paul's school have been developing aspects of his thought, and this sets an early date. An outer limit can be established by the fact that the letter to the Ephesians made use of the letter to the Colossians.

Where was the letter to the Colossians written? The fact that the letter to the Colossians is closely tied to the letter to Philemon may mean that Ephesus is where the letter to the Colossians was written. Paul asked Philemon for a guest room (Philem. 22), and this is more easily explained if Paul was imprisoned in Ephesus than Rome, because such a request from Rome would imply that Paul had abandoned or deferred his trip to Spain. That Paul had a large number of fellow workers around him in prison is more easily explained in Ephesus than Caesarea. The Marcionite prologue to the letter to the Colossians states that Paul wrote it from Ephesus.

2 THESSALONIANS

2 Thessalonians was the first letter bearing Paul's name which prompted interpreters to question its Pauline authorship since the beginning of the nineteenth century. While some regarded 2 Thessalonians as a pseudonymous writing, another group of interpreters safeguarded Pauline authorship in a variety of ways. For instance, the suggestion of Hugo Grotius (1640) that 2 Thessalonians might have been written prior to 1 Thessalonians has found quite a few adherents in the twentieth century (e.g., T. W. Manson; Hurd, IDB Supplement), but this hypothesis comes to nought on 1 Thess. 2:17–3:6 which clearly implies that 1 Thessalonians is Paul's first letter to that church.

Adolf von Harnack tried to show that 2 Thessalonians had originally been addressed only to the Jewish Christian minority of Thessalonica, whereas 1 Thessalonians was to be read by the whole church. However, it seems improbable that Paul who vigorously combatted factionalism would have acquiesced to it in Thessalonica by writing to one group in the community without exhorting that group to unity. Recognizing this difficulty, Martin Dibelius suggested that 1 Thessalonians was meant for the leaders of that church while 2 Thessalonians was addressed to the whole community. But this theory falters on 1 Thess. 5:27 which demands that "this letter be read to all brothers." One also would have to ask why the admonition to respect the community leaders (1 Thess. 5:12) is found in the letter addressed to these leaders and not in the letter to the whole church.

Another alternative was proposed by Eduard Schweizer which would answer the problem why Paul would write two such similar and yet in some aspects strikingly different letters to the same community within a short period. Schweizer suggested that 2 Thessalonians was originally a letter addressed to the church in Philippi. In support he cites Polycarp of Smyrna who in his letter to the Philippians (Pol. Phil. 3:2) speaks of Pauline letters (plural) to the Philippians. Furthermore, Polycarp seems to allude to 2 Thess. 1:4 and 3:15 (Pol. Phil. 11:3, 4). However, 2 Thess. 2:15 implies the reception of a prior letter and this letter could not have been Philippians because 2 Thess. 2:1 ("in connection with our being gathered to him") refers back to a similar phrase in 1 Thess. 4:17.

Schmithals approached the problem of 2 Thessalonians from another angle. On the basis of its two thanksgivings (1:3–12 and 2:13 f.) and its two exhortations (2:15–3:5 and 3:6–15) he concluded that 2 Thessalonians is a composite epistle consisting of two originally separate Pauline letters. One letter is comprised of 1:1–12, 3:6–16; the other is comprised of 2:13–14, 2:1–12, 2:15–3:5, 3:17–18. This theory did not commend itself because the first "letter" would lack a body and 3:6–16 could hardly be the continuation of the thanksgiving.

The variety of ways in which scholars sought to uphold Pauline authorship and simultaneously deal with individual problems raised by this letter indicates that 2 Thessalonians is indeed a tough nut to crack. However, the lack of any satisfactory solution which could gain widespread acceptance did not result in agreement on the pseudonymity of 2 Thessalonians. On the contrary, almost all commentaries produced in this century on 2 Thessalonians are written from the perspective of its Pauline authorship, and according to the traditional viewpoint, namely, that Paul wrote this letter within a short time after 1 Thessalonians. This traditional viewpoint is unsatisfactory because of the following four problems.

THE ESCHATOLOGY OF 2 THESSALONIANS AS PROBLEM

The problem does not lie primarily in the concepts found in 2 Thess. 2:1–10 which are absent in all other letters bearing Paul's name; nor does it lie in the fact that the End appears suddenly and unexpectedly in 1 Thessalonians while in 2 Thessalonians it appears in connection with signs. The problem lies in the *direction* in which the eschatological argument of 2:1–10 points the reader—a direction which is the very opposite from that found in 1 Thess. 4:13–5:11. In 1 Thessalonians Paul emphasized the imminence of Christ's parousia (1 Thess. 4:15, 17; 5:1–5), an emphasis which reoccurs also in Paul's later letters. "The Lord is at hand" (Phil. 4:5; 1 Cor. 7:29, 31; Rom. 13:11–12). This means that from his first to his last extant letter the apostle held fast to the expectation of the imminent End, even though in Philippians he recognized the possibility that he himself might "die and be with Christ" (Phil. 1:23). But precisely the eschatological direction toward the imminent End is reversed in 2 Thess. 2:1–10. Before the Day of the Lord comes there must first take place a series of events, the apostasy, the manifestation of the Rebel, and before these can take place, there must be the disappearance of the *katechon*, whatever and whoever that might be. It ought to be obvious that the delay of the parousia functions as the presupposition of the argumentation of 2 Thessalonians 2 and it is the emphasis on the distance of the eschaton which gives the direction to the eschatological timetable of this chapter. The change in the direction of the eschatological argument, rather than the new concepts introduced in this chapter, makes Pauline authorship of 2 Thessalonians improbable. Thus far, the defenders of Pauline authorship have failed to explain why Paul, when he had to deal with eschatological enthusiasm subsequently (Philippians, 1 Corinthians), continued the direction of his eschatology found in 1 Thessalonians and did not take up the thrust of 2 Thessalonians 2.

It is an oversimplification of the problem to argue that in 1 Thessalonians Paul suggested that the End is near, while in 2 Thessalonians he showed that it had not yet arrived. This line of interpretation misses the eschatological directions of 1 and 2 Thessalonians and does not perceive that the distance of the parousia is presupposed in 2 Thessalonians and that precisely this distance is un-Pauline. Occasionally, upholders of Pauline authorship have concluded on the basis of 1:7 that also our letter affirms Paul's expectancy of the imminent End. In 1:7 we read that God deems it just "to grant peace *together with us* to you." This verse is taken by some (e.g., Jewett) to express Paul's hope of being alive at Christ's parousia (cf. 1 Thess. 4:15, 17). But such an interpretation ignores the trend of thought in 2 Thess. 1:5–7. The living are here not contrasted with those who have died as is the case in 1 Thess. 4:15. 2 Thess. 1:7 states that the readers and the author will be sharing the future eschatological gift of peace because in the present they are enduring suffering (1:5). V. 5 should read "for which you *also* are suffering." The "also" is wrongly omitted in the RSV. It implies that suffering is experienced not just by the persons addressed but also by the writer of this letter. 2 Thess. 1:5–7 contrasts present suffering with future peace and expresses the solidarity of the readers and the author in both time dimensions. It cannot be used to demonstrate the presence of the Pauline expectation of the imminent parousia and thus the authenticity of this letter.

On the contrary, 2 Thess. 2:2 f. disputes the legitimacy of the hope of the imminence of Christ's parousia. Those who uphold it are thought by our writer to be "unreasonable," "shaken out of their mind" (2:2), and the readers are solemnly warned not to permit any talk about the presence or the imminence of the eschaton to "deceive" them (2:3). We will deal later on with the meaning of the sentence "the Day of the Lord has come" (2:2), but here it suffices to point out that the Thessalonian troublemakers did not claim that Christ's parousia had come and with it the resurrection of the dead. No one claimed that the living had already been "caught up" together with the resurrected believers "to meet Christ in the air" (1 Thess. 4:17). Hence, the *meaning* of the sentence, "the Day of the Lord" has come, is that Christ's parousia is imminent. That notion is denounced by our writer as deceit. Therefore, the author of our letter can hardly be Paul, for whom Christ "is at hand" (Phil. 4:5; 1 Thess. 4:13). It would appear that a pupil of Paul modified Paul's eschatology for a new situation.

Advocates of the pseudonymity of 2 Thessalonians have frequently argued that the *signs* prior to the eschaton found in 2 Thessalonians 2 are incompatible with Paul's announcement that the End will come *suddenly* and *unexpectedly* (1 Thess. 5:1 f.). Against this approach it has rightly been pointed out that Jewish and Christian apocalypses contain both motifs side by side (e.g., Mark 13:33 where the End comes suddenly; Mark 13:7–25 where the End comes after signs). However, we might rightly ask whether the apocalypses which contain these two motifs of signs and suddenness are not the end product of the fusion of two originally separate traditions—one tradition which spoke of the End in terms of suddenness, the other which spoke of it in terms of signs. Turning to Paul, it would seem that if he had actually instructed the Thessalonians on the appearance of anti-Christ after the disappearance of the *katechon*, as claimed in 2 Thess. 2:5, then Paul must have forgotten that instruction when he wrote 1 Thess. 5:1 f. But also the Thessalonians must have forgotten his instruction when they accepted the notion that the Day of the Lord is present. We might ask, is it probable that Paul might have given them oral instructions on the anti-Christ, the apostasy, and the *katechon* when we know from 1 Thess. 4:13 f. that he had not yet instructed them on the subject of the resurrection of believers who had died? While the motifs of signs and suddenness are found alongside each other in Christian apocalypses, in the Pauline corpus the motif of signs is found only in 2 Thessalonians. Other Pauline letters have the motif of suddenness. Nowhere else did Paul speak of the anti-Christ, the apostasy, and the *katechon*. In conclusion, neither the direction of the eschatological argument in 2 Thessalonians nor its concepts serve as the basis for the eschatology found in later Pauline letters. Nor can 2 Thessalonians 2 be regarded as a further development of the eschatology as found in 1 Thessalonians. The eschatology of 2 Thessalonians suggests that its author is someone other than the apostle Paul.

LITERARY PROBLEMS

The warning against the imminent End expectancy has not been the sole ground for objecting to the Pauline authorship of this letter. Equally important are such literary matters as resemblance in *structure, verbal parallels, non-Pauline stylistic elements,* and *lack of concrete personal data.* If these items are viewed separately, in isolation from each other, one might be tempted to dismiss them. Viewed together they become a strong argument for assuming the pseudonymity of 2 Thessalonians.

In their present form both Thessalonian letters contain two thanksgivings (1 Thess. 1:2–10; 2:13–16; 2 Thess. 1:3–12; 2:13 f.) These twofold thanksgivings differ from all other letters under Paul's name. To be sure, Paul Schubert had claimed that 1 Thessalonians contains only one thanksgiving which begins in 1:2 and ends in 3:13. But further work has clearly shown, first of all, that 1 Thess. 2:13 does indeed begin a second thanksgiving, and, second, the content of this second thanksgiving is un-Pauline. In short, 1 Thess. 2:13 f. constitutes an interpolation into a Pauline text. (C. Pearson, HTR 64, 1971, 79–94; Boers, NTS 22, 1976, 151–152.)

A few comments on 1 Thess. 2:13 might be in order. This text flies not only in the face of Romans 9–11 and of 1 Thess. 3:12 where the readers are enjoined to love not just one another, but "all men," which presumably includes Jews, but it is contrary to the basic structure of Paul's letters which have only one thanksgiving. The opening words of 1 Thess. 2:13, "and on account of this we too" give thanks, seem to indicate that there are also other people besides Paul who give thanks, but in fact none are mentioned beforehand. The phrase, "on account of this," refers not backwards, but forward and gives the reason why "we too" give thanks, namely, because "you received the word . . . for you became imitators of the churches of Judea . . . for you suffered . . . as they did from the *Jews* who," etc. In short, it should not be denied that 1 Thess. 2:13–16 constitutes in its present form and position a second thanksgiving, and thus it is automatically suspect on formal grounds. The climax of this thanksgiving and thus the very reason for introducing a second thanksgiving is the series of ugly anti-Semitic, or, better, anti-Jewish statements. These anti-Jewish statements are already cast in the form of a fixed tradition which is based not on inner Jewish criticisms but on pagan anti-Jewish polemics as found in Hellenistic Roman writers of that period. The climax of the thanksgiving is that "God's wrath has come upon them at last." This final sentence (2:16) refers to a past event. But there is no event in first century history to which 1 Thess. 2:16 would apply except the Jewish war against Rome or the destruction of Jerusalem by Rome. We therefore regard 1 Thess. 2:16 as an interpolation. We might also note the statement in 2:15 that the Jews "killed" Jesus—a statement which is simply not true. A closer look at this section would bring to light other oddities, such as the notion of the imitation of communities and the vehemence of language which is out of place since it is not Jews but gentiles who have caused the Christians in Thessalonica to suffer. In conclusion, on formal and internal grounds this anti-Jewish vendetta cloaked in the form of a thanksgiving to God should be regarded as an interpolation even as 1 Cor. 14:13b–36 or 2 Cor. 6:14–7:1 are interpolations into Pauline letters. If this second thanksgiving is omitted the structure of 1 Thessalonians becomes clear. Prescript; thanksgiving: 1:2–10; apology of the apostolic ministry: 2:1–12; the apostolic parousia: 2:17–3:13; exhortations and instructions: 4:1–5:22; closing: 5:22–28.

If the second thanksgiving in 1 Thessalonians is an interpolation, then the presence of a second thanksgiving in 2 Thess. 2:13 at once casts doubt upon the Pauline authorship of this letter. We conclude that 2 Thess. 2:13 f. is an imitation of the structure of two thanksgivings found by the author of 2 Thessalonians in the interpolated form of 1 Thessalonians. As in the present interpolated form of 1 Thessalonians so here the second thanksgiving (2:13) opens a new section which closes with a benediction (3:5).

Our writer did not wish to deal with the theme of the apostolic ministry (1 Thess. 2:1–12) or with the theme of the apostolic parousia (1 Thess. 2:17–3:11). Therefore he moved his teaching concerning the eschaton (par. 1 Thess. 4:13–5:11) forward, placing it between the two thanksgivings. Otherwise the second thanksgiving would have followed immediately upon the first. However, in 2 Thess. 2:1–12 our author retained the hortatory frame in which Paul's doctrinal teaching of 1 Thess. 4:13 had been placed (see 1 Thess. 4:1 and 2 Thess. 2:1—"we beg you brothers").

Thus the following outline for 2 Thessalonians emerges.

Prescript. 1:1–2.
Thanksgiving. 1:3–12. The prayer of 1:11 marks the transition.
  I) 2:1–12. Eschatological doctrine framed as exhortation.
 II) 2:13–3:5. Thanksgiving, admonition, benediction.
    First cycle.   A) 2:13–14. Thanksgiving.
                  B) 2:15. Direct admonition.
                  C) 2:16. Benediction.
    Second cycle. A) 3:1–2. Request for intercession.
                  B) 3:3–4. Indirect admonition.
                  C) 3:5. Benediction.
III) 3:6–16. Admonitions.
  A) 3:6–12. Ordinance against the disorderly and idlers.
  B) 3:13–15. General admonition of faithful members.
Closing. 3:16–18.
  A) 3:16. Benediction of peace.
  B) 3:17. Greetings.
  C) 3:18. Benediction of grace.

The structure of this letter is remarkable. On one hand it shows imitation of the twofold thanksgiving of 1 Thessalonians, and on the other hand part II with its two cycles closing with two benedictions has no parallel in other Pauline letters. The address, "Brothers," (1:3; 2:1, 13, 15; 3:1, 6, 13) indicates the beginnings of new sections with the exception of 2:15. There it indicates the programmatic significance of this verse which contains the basic exhortation and the first explicit imperative. We might also note that in distinction to Pauline thanksgivings the address, "Brothers," has become part of the introductory thanksgiving formula of 2 Thessalonians. The benedictions (2:16; 3:6) imitate the benediction of 1 Thess. 3:12–13 in structure and occasional wording.

Turning to the *vocabulary, phrases,* and *style* of 2 Thessalonians, we note a vast number of words from 1 Thessalonians reappearing in 2 Thessalonians, occasionally even in the same sequence. This prompted W. Wrede to argue for a literary dependence of our letter on 1 Thessalonians and hence for pseudonymous authorship. However, other interpreters like Rigaux used the same data to argue in favor of Pauline authorship, adding that our letter must have been written in immediate proximity to 1 Thessalonians when the vocabulary of the latter was still in Paul's mind. While the case for literary dependence has not been successfully made, we note that the case in favor of Pauline authorship based on similarity of language evaporates when the verbal similarities are placed alongside an abundance of un-Pauline language found in 2 Thessalonians. Moreover, the absence of typically Pauline stylistic features (e.g., the style of the diatribe) and the presence of stylistic features absent in 1 Thessalonians point to a post-Pauline origin of our letter, to an origin in a Pauline circle which knew 1 Thessalonians, tended to and further developed Paul's language, molding it into idiomatic elements and theological cliches.

1. Some examples of *similarity* of langauge which also exhibit differences: The prescript (1:1–2) in its first two parts is exactly the same as in 1 Thessalonians 1. The phrase, the church "in God," is found in Pauline prescripts only in these two letters. Other prescripts do not speak of the Philippians or Corinthians but use the name of the city. This similarity of language is surprising in view of the variety which Paul employs in his other prescripts. Therefore, the difference in the salutation (1:2) is all the more significant because it brings the expanded form found in later

letters. This expansion upsets the balance between the individual parts of the prescript as found in 1 Thessalonians and, moreover, it repeats the "God (our) Father and the Lord Jesus Christ." This repetition is in agreement with the writer's fondness for synonymous parallelisms to which we shall turn later.

The salutation is followed by the customary thanksgiving, expressed in a way found nowhere else in Paul. 2 Thess. 1:5–10 seems to be a tradition about the apocalyptic reversal which our writer incorporated into his thanksgiving. Yet the thanksgiving of 2 Thessalonians has many parallels of language with 1 Thessalonians, e.g., "work of faith," (1:11; 1 Thess. 1:3); faith, love . . . endurance (1:3 f.; 1 Thess. 1:3); the gentiles "who do not know God" (1:8; 1 Thess. 4:5). Though the words are identical in each case, the meaning is slightly different. "Endurance" in 2 Thessalonians refers to endurance under persecution; those who do not know God are not the immoral pagans but persecutors. The transition to the main topic, "now we beg you, brothers," (2:1) is found in 1 Thess. 4:1; 5:12, but otherwise only in Phil. 4:3. While the section 2:1–12 contains the main theme and the chief reason for this letter, we note the flashback in 2:5 which is parallel to 1 Thess. 3:4. The second thanksgiving and prayer (2:13–17) re-echoes several characteristic words and ideas scattered throughout 1 Thessalonians. The prayer of 2:17 is found in the same position as the prayer of 1 Thess. 3:11, while the prayer of 3:5, "the Lord direct your hearts," may be compared with 1 Thess. 3:11, "God direct our way," the only Pauline texts which contain the verb *kateuthynein*. Note also the use of optatives in 2:16; 3:5, 16; 1 Thess. 3:11 f.; 5:23. Both hortatory sections begin with "finally" (3:1; 1 Thess. 4:1) which is used rarely by Paul as a transitional particle. Turning to the hortatory section, we shall compare 3:8 with 1 Thess. 2:9 which have in common the words "toil" and "labor," "we worked night and day that we might not burden any of you." Also this example shows the use of the same words, but their thrust is different. Only in 2 Thess. 3:7–10 do we find the notion that the *purpose* of Paul's lifestyle was to give believers an example to imitate. Last, both letters close with a prayer that begins "Now may the Lord (God) of peace" (3:16; 1 Thess. 5:23).

The similarity of words and phrases between the two Thessalonian letters might indeed indicate that Paul wrote our letter shortly after 1 Thessalonians. However, the presence of un-Pauline cliches, the abundance of synonymous parallelisms, and the absence of typically Pauline stylistic features argue against Pauline authorship of 2 Thessalonians.

2. Some examples of un-Pauline stereotyped language: "We are bound to give thanks as it is fitting" (1:3; 2:13); "the gospel of our Lord Jesus" (1:8); "inflicting vengeance" (1:8); "to suffer punishment" (1:9); "eternal destruction" (1:9); "our witness" (1:10); "decision for goodness" (1:11); "to be shaken in mind" (2:2); "the mystery of rebellion" (2:7); "to be out of the way" (2:7); "the manifestation of his parousia" (2:8); "the love of the truth" (2:10); "the deceit of wickedness" (2:10); "the power of delusion" (2:11); "to believe the truth" (2:12); "sanctification by the Spirit" (2:13); "faith in the truth" (2:13); "eternal encouragement" (*paraklēsis*—2:16); "good hope" (2:16); "God our Father" (two articles—2:16); "to speed on and be glorified" (3:1); "wicked and evil" (3:2); "the endurance of Christ" (3:5); "to walk in idleness" (3:6, 11); "the Lord of peace" (3:16). None of these phrases are found otherwise in Paul and with the exception of "sanctification by the Spirit" (2:13), they do not occur in the rest of the NT.

3. Examples of *parallelism* in 2 Thessalonians: These examples are all the more important when we recognize their sparsity in 1 Thessalonians. For the following see Trilling.

> Your faith grows abundantly
> and the love of each one of you increases (1:3).
> To repay tribulation to those who cause you tribulation
> and [to repay] peace to you who suffer tribulation (1:6).
> To those who do not know God
> and do not obey the gospel of our Lord Jesus (1:8).
> From the presence of the Lord
> and from the glory of his might (1:9).
> To be glorified among the saints
> and to be marvelled at among all who believe (1:10).
> That God may make you worthy of his call
> and may accomplish every resolve for goodness (1:11).
> Concerning the parousia of our Lord
> and our being gathered to him (2:1).
> First the apostasy takes place
> and the man of rebellion is revealed (2:3).
> Him the Lord will slay with the breath of his mouth
> and will destroy by the manifestation of his parousia (2:8).
> Those who have not believed the truth
> but had pleasure in unrighteousness (2:12).
> Who has loved us
> and has given us eternal encouragement (2:16).

Additional examples may be found in Trilling (pp. 52 f.).

The recognition of this parallelism style in 2 Thessalonians is important for the interpreter. For instance, the assertion that the Lord and God the Father "has loved us" does not refer to Christ's cross as is the case otherwise in Paul's letters, but to the "eternal comfort" in the midst of distress, and to the good hope that points to Christ's ultimate victory and the readers' glory. Most of the above parallelisms appear to be formulaic idioms and not on-the-spot formulations. They give a ponderous tone to our letter and point to the post-Pauline origin of this writing.

4. The *stylistic difference* is also apparent when we recognize Paul's fondness for triadic formulations in 1 Thessalonians and their almost total absence in 2 Thessalonians where we find only one traditional triadic phrase: "with all power (singular) and with . . . signs and wonders" (2:9).

Above all, we must recognize the absence of typically Pauline rhetoric in 2 Thessalonians. While 1 Thessalonians has the characteristic of Pauline speech, committed to writing, 2 Thessalonians reads, as Rigaux aptly remarked, like a "papal encyclica." Hence the feature of the diatribe is absent and we could identify 2 Thessalonians as a treatise in the form of a letter. This would also explain the absence of Paul's travel plans in 2 Thessalonians and the often observed coolness of the author to his readers, in spite of 2 Thess. 1:3, which speaks of their abundant growth of faith. The traditional psychological interpretation which sees in Paul's coolness the result of his disappointment with the idlers does not take cognizance of 2 Thess. 1:3.

THEOLOGICAL PROBLEMS

In addition to the eschatology there are other theological items which put Pauline authorship of this letter in question. 2 Thessalonians frequently substitutes the title "Lord" meaning Jesus where in 1 Thessalonians we find "God" (2 Thess. 2:13, 16; 3:1, 3, 5, 16). The "beloved by God" of 1 Thess. 1:4 become "beloved by the Lord" in 2 Thess. 2:13. Such a replacement, especially in contexts of prayer, points to a liturgical usage which is typical of the post-Pauline period.

Striking is the absence of the motif of "joy" which is so important in Paul's description of the eschatological existence of life in Christ. Equally important is the absence of the kerygma of the cross and the resurrection in this writing. In 1 Thessalonians Paul unfolded the theme of eschatology on the basis of the creed: "We believe that Jesus died and rose again" (1 Thess. 4:14). In 2 Thessalonians the kerygma of the cross and resurrection has disappeared beneath the horizon and the OT doctrine of divine retribution against the persecutors of God's people has come to the fore. To be sure, Paul can also speak of God's judgment (2 Cor. 5:10; Rom. 2:5–6), but nowhere does the apostle use the idea of divine retribution in order to *comfort* believers in distress. Parallel to the absence of the Pauline theology of the cross and resurrection is the dearth of language about the Spirit. In 2:2 "pneuma" means the inspired pronouncement by a particular Christian prophet. In 2:8 we hear of the divine Spirit—breath—with which Christ destroys the Rebel at his parousia. In 2:13 we find the cliché "sanctification by the Spirit" which is unknown otherwise in Paul's letters, but appears in 1 Pet. 1:2. If we compare 1 Thess. 1:5, 6; 4:8; 5:19, 23 with 2 Thess. 2:13 then the poverty of our letter's pneumatology becomes obvious. "Sanctification by the Spirit" (2:13) is paralleled with "belief in the truth," that is, belief in the kind of orthodoxy set forth in 2 Thessalonians, an orthodoxy that includes the proper apocalyptic timetable.

Turning to the exhortations in 2 Thess. 3:6 f., we note that Paul's idea that an exemplary Christian lifestyle functions as witness and service to unbelievers (1 Thess. 4:12; 5:15) is absent. On the other hand we find the un-Pauline idea that the *purpose* of Paul's lifestyle is to give an example which *must* (*dei*) be imitated. (Compare 1 Thess. 1:6 f. with 2 Thess. 3:7–9.) In 2 Thessalonians the idea of imitation of the apostle refers to his work and not to his suffering in the service of Christ.

In conclusion, the literary problems and the theological problems encountered in this letter point to a non-Pauline authorship.

THE PSEUDONYMOUS LETTER AND
THE SIGN OF AUTHENTICITY

There are a total of four explicit references to a "letter" in 2 Thessalonians (2:2, 15; 3:14, 17) and each one of them poses a problem. The RSV translation "by letter purporting to be from us" (2:2) could be an over-translation. Furthermore, the Greek phrase *hōs di hēmōn* may be connected not just with letter, but also with "spirit and word" or with "word and letter." In view of the reference to "word of mouth or letter" in 2:15, we choose the last alternative.

Grammatically, the phrase *hōs di hēmōn* may indicate not the presence of non-Pauline sources, but the presence of a misinterpretation of Paul's oral or written statements to support the false view that "the Day of the Lord has come." The phrase *hōs di hēmōn* would then be translated "as coming from us" and it would not imply the existence of a pseudonymous letter, but would refer to a wrong interpretation of oral or written statements by Paul. However, if Paul had actually thought that the Thessalonians had misunderstood or misinterpreted his eschatology as set forth in his oral proclamation and in 1 Thessalonians, we would expect him to re-define his position as he did in similar situations (see 1 Cor. 5:9–13). He could, for instance, have asked, "Have you Thessalonians already been 'caught up' and have you 'met the Lord in the air' (1 Thess. 4:17)? Have your dead already 'been raised' (1 Thess. 4:16)? If not, how can you talk about the presence of the eschaton in an ultimate way?" Hence it is unconvincing that Paul shortly after the writing of 1 Thessalonians sought to correct a misunderstanding caused by that letter.

If we assume the author of 2 Thessalonians to be someone other than Paul, then the translation "a letter purporting to come from us" could refer to 1 Thessalonians. In that case, we would encounter the spectacle that a pseudonymous Paulinist would try his best to degrade an authentic letter of Paul, namely, 1 Thessalonians into a pseudonymous one. Simultaneously, our author claims apostolic authorship for his own work (see also 2 Thess. 3:17). This position is taken in a recent article (ZNW 1977, 35–47). Obviously, our author did not reach his first goal, though he accomplished his second. However, 1 Thessalonians contains neither the sentence nor the idea that the Day of the Lord is already present—except in the interpolation of 2:13–16. Moreover, the linguistic parallels between 1 and 2 Thessalonians would seem to demonstrate that our author regarded 1 Thessalonians as Pauline and 2 Thess. 2:15 supports that conclusion.

This leaves us with the alternative that in 2:2 either Paul himself separated himself from a pseudonymous letter or a later Paulinist did so. Against the former view we note a twofold difficulty. First, the assumption of the circulation of pseudonymous Pauline writings during the apostle's own lifetime is problematic. We must keep in mind the shortness of the time between the founding of the

church in Thessalonica (probably fall A.D. 49) and the writing of
1 Thessalonians (probably spring A.D. 50). If 2 Thessalonians is
from Paul it has to follow a few weeks later. It is unlikely that
during that brief span of time a pseudonymous Pauline letter would
make its appearance. The age of Christian pseudonymity and
anonymity is the period between A.D. 70 and A.D. 110. Second,
equally puzzling would be the absence of polemics by Paul against
an actual or a supposed forgery in his name. We can be rea-
sonably certain that Paul would have been vocal in his denunciation
if he had known or supposed that in his name his beloved Thessalonians had been deceived by "word or letter."

In light of this we propose that the phrase *hōs di hēmōn* (2:2)
indeed was meant to refer to a pseudonymous Pauline pronouncement and to a pseudonymous Pauline letter. Since the existence
of pseudonymous writings during Paul's lifetime is improbable,
we conclude that 2:2 is an indication of the pseudonymity of 2
Thessalonians. Our author subtly polemicizes against a pseudonymous Pauline writing and another Pauline group. In order to
have his own writing accepted as apostolic writing our author used
a trick in 3:17. It has often been pointed out that "the mark of
every letter of mine; this is the way I write" (3:17) is appropriate in a first letter to a church. After all, in subsequent letters the
readers already know his handwriting in which he conveyed his
greetings. Moreover if "every" Pauline letter is recognizable by
Paul's own handwriting ("this is the way I write"), then any
appeal to a pseudonymous Pauline letter would be rather futile
so long as the original letter bearing greetings in Paul's own handwriting was still in existence. Hence we conclude that 2 Thessalonians belongs to a time and place where the Pauline letters were
available only in the form of copies. In conclusion, the cumula-
tive effect of these four problems prompts us to regard 2 Thessalonians as a pseudonymous writing.

SITUATION

Both our author and his opponent were Paulinists—both
claimed Paul's authority—and both employed the literary device
of pseudonymity. Yet our author did not hereticize his opponent.

No anathemas were hurled at him, though he warned his reader, "Let no one deceive you in any way" (2:3).

In this letter we gain a brief glimpse into tensions that existed in a post-Pauline community. Under the leadership of a Christian prophet and on the basis of a pseudonymous Pauline letter a group within the community affirmed the presence of the eschaton. We would probably not go too far afield if we assigned the interpolation of 1 Thess. 2:13–16 to this particular group which taught that "the Day of the Lord has come." Jewish apocalypticism lent the tools to their interpretation of history and articulated the Chrisian experience of suffering (1 Thess. 2:14; 2 Thess. 1:4–10). Jersualem's fate of A.D. 70 was viewed by them as the inbreaking of God's ultimate judgment (1 Thess. 2:16). If the wrath of God has already come upon the Jews (*eis telos*) and the Christians already experience the messianic woes in their suffering (2 Thess. 1:4), then the conclusion could be drawn that "the Day of the Lord is present" (2:2c). Against this background our letter is written in order to give directions to Christians "shaken in mind and excited" (2:2a).

There is a second concrete problem to which our letter speaks and which may have been connected with the excitement concerning the presence of the eschaton even though our author does not make this connection explicit. In 3:6–12 we hear warnings against idleness and polemics against loafers who "do not work." They are commanded to labor with "calmness, earning their own keep" (3:12). It is possible that those loafers shunned work because manual labor was viewed with distaste among Greeks or perhaps they thought that their new status as children of God gave them the right to live as parasites from the community. It is equally possible that the apocalyptic excitement produced these loafers who are simultaneously called "busybodies" (3:11) and exhorted to quiet calmness (3:12). These loafers could well have argued—why work since the Day of the Lord is present already?

Some interpreters (Marxsen, Jewett) try to show that the recipients of 2 Thessalonians had fallen prey to Hellenistic Gnosticism, to the kind of realized eschatology which found expression in the slogan: "Our resurrection has happened already" (2 Tim. 2:18). A Gnosticizing interpretation of the opponents of 2 Thessalonians is undoubtedly incorrect because it misses the theme of the letter, announced in the first thanksgiving, which is persecution and apocalyptic expectations. The opponents are not proto-Gnostics but rather apocalyptic enthusiasts.

THE MESSAGE

The tenses of the verbs in 1:4–6 clearly indicate that the recipients of our letter were being subjected to persecution. We do not know which form that persecution took, but persecutions may range from verbal abuse to harrassment, ostracism, occasional beatings, imprisonment, and even worse. We may assume that not all members suffered the same intensity of abuse as some did, though all felt the pressure of the world. We may also assume that these afflictions produced a crisis within the community. The first thing which our author did was to emphasize the necessity and propriety of giving thanks to God within this context of persecution and affliction. That thanksgiving is not man's normal response in the situation of suffering is rather obvious, but our author states his reasons for giving thanks to God quite clearly. Their faith and their love have not ceased, but have grown (1:3). Moreover, our author indicates that their suffering is not pointless, but has eternal significance in that they are suffering for the kingdom of God (1:5). He comforts his readers with the assurance of God's vindication "in the revelation of the Lord Jesus Christ from heaven" (1:7) who will bring about the apocalyptic reversal of persecutor and persecuted (1:7–10).

Form critically, vv. 5–10 are a thematic expansion of the Pauline thanksgiving designed to give consolation to oppressed Christians by reminding them of God's eschatological judgment which is yet to come. Grammatically, these verses are awkward and Dibelius is probably correct in his suggestion that our author made use of a Hellenistic Jewish apocalyptic text to which he added the following: "That you may be made worthy of the kingdom of God for which you are suffering" (v. 5)—"with us" (v. 7)—"Jesus" (v. 7) —"and upon those who do not obey the gospel of our Lord Jesus"

(v. 8)—"because our testimony to you was believed" (v. 10). With these additions, our author Christianized his tradition.

Negatively, the judgment theophany implies that according to our author the final judgment is yet to come and the sufferings of the present time do not usher in the Day of the Lord, nor are they signs of the presence of that day. We must assume that the author's opponents interpreted their tribulations as messianic woes which either bring about or are part of the Day of the Lord. This idea has not only Jewish antecedents but found expression in different ways in the NT. In 1 Peter the "fiery ordeal" consists in "the sufferings of *the* Christ" which believers endure in the present and which mark the kairos of the beginning of the final judgment (1 Pet. 4:12, 13, 17). While our author did not minimize the significance of the present suffering, he rejected its interpretation in terms of the messianic woes. He is therefore more in tune with Luke's eschatology than with 1 Pet. 4:12–17.

The most important section and the primary reason for writing this letter is the little apocalypse of 2:1–12. Its purpose is to demonstrate that the Day of the Lord is not present and simultaneously to give consolation and hope by pointing to Christ's inevitable, ultimate victory over all satanic forces.

The question which has been debated at length whether the Greek verb *enestēken* should be translated as "is present" or "is imminent" is actually less important than the recognition of the context within which that statement occurs. The perfect participle of this verb usually means "present." Occasionally it can be used to indicate that something is imminent or impending (1 Cor. 7:26). Hence it is the linguistic context which must elucidate the meaning of the verb. The pseudo-Paulinists, against whom this chapter seeks to give direction, regarded their present persecution as part of the beginning of the Day of the Lord. That day is therefore not a twenty-four hour day, but the eschaton beginning with the messianic woes and climaxing with Christ's victory over all hostile forces. Hence the translation "is present," "has arrived," "has come" is indeed proper, so long as we remember that those Paulinists did not claim that the resurrection of the dead had already occurred. With respect to the resurrection, the meaning of *enestēken* would be "is imminent," is "impending."

With his apocalypse, our writer taught that the Day of the Lord will come only if three prior conditions have been fulfilled. 1) The rebellion—the *apostasia*—must come first (2:3). 2) The opponent of God and of all religion must make his parousia and by the activity of Satan "in all power with signs and wonders" deceive those who are to perish (2:3–4, 9–10). 3) Before the counter-God can make his appearance there must occur a disappearance of something and someone which is active in the present and which our author calls *to katechon* (neuter) and *ho katechōn* (masculine) and which the recipients *know* (2:5–7).

The notions of an eschatological apostasy and of an eschatological agent of Satan were taken over by Christians from Jewish apocalypticism (Jub. 23:14 f.; 4 Ezra 5:1 f.; 1QHAB 2:1 f.; Jude 17-Dan. 11:36). It is difficult to say whether our *author* believed that the church itself would be involved in apostasy. 2 Thess. 1:3–4 and 2:13 f. would speak against it. Perhaps our author thought that the church will encounter apostasy primarily as a threat or that the apostasy would be a Jewish affair. Pagans by definition "do not know God" (1:8) and hence can hardly be thought to apostatize unless for our author apostasy would include the forsaking of pagan worship for the sake of adhering to the Rebel. But these questions are peripheral to our writer's real concern. The point he wishes to make is that the Day of the Lord is not present because the present is determined by the *katechon* and by "the mystery of rebellion." The future will bring the apostasy and the manifestation of the Rebel. Only then comes the parousia of Christ and with it the Day of the Lord.

The reference to the temple in 2:4 does not demonstrate that our letter was written prior to A.D. 70, and, hence, by Paul, contrary to J. A. T. Robinson (*Redating the New Testament*, 1976, p. 53 f.), because: 1) the defilement of the temple was an apocalyptic theme (Mark 13:14; Dan. 11:31, 36) which was used by apocalyptic writers also after A.D. 70 (Rev. 11:1; Asc. Isa. 4:11). 2) It is by no means certain that our author in distinction to his tradition meant the temple shrine in Jerusalem. He could have used it metaphorically as equivalent to "proclaiming himself to be God" without thinking of a particular location. 3) Equally important in this connection is the probability that also after A.D. 70 temple worship took place in Jerusalem (*NTS* 6, 1960, 269–280).

The idea that the temple of 2:4 refers to the heavenly sanctuary coming down to earth has even less to commend itself than the suggestion that the temple of God is the church of God. In that case, the apostasy would take place within the church.

While it is possible that in agreement with his tradition our author believed that at some future date a self-deifying figure of universal significance would proclaim himself to be God in Jerusalem's temple, it is equally possible that he did not reflect on the locale, but made use of traditional material. Nor did he reflect on the Jewish or pagan origin of the Rebel who brings about the eschatological apostasy. For him it was self-evident that his readers would recognize him when he made his appearance in the future.

We should notice the absence of two otherwise characteristic traits of apocalyptic Jewish anti-God figures. First, nothing is said about the persecution of the people of God by the Rebel, in distinction to Revelation 13 and 17. Second, unlike the anti-God figure of Dan. 11:31 and 36, the Rebel of our chapter bears no royal traits. He is not pictured as a latter day Antiochus Epiphanes, but as a satanic miracle worker, a deceiver and self-exalter. The reasons for this picture of the Rebel are not hard to find. We have pointed out repeatedly that the readers are already under persecution and that some of them regarded their trials as evidence of the presence of the eschaton. Our author would hardly give consolation to his readers and calm their already unsettled minds if he were to tell them that their present persecutions are merely a prelude to still greater persecutions yet to come. Hence he did not portary the Rebel as an imperial persecutor of the elect but rather as a universal, self-deifying, miracle working deceiver.

By means of the concepts of the *katechon* and "the mystery of rebellion" he linked his readers' present time with the future manifestation of the Rebel (2:6–7). These verses are among the most difficult and disputed within the NT. Besides obscure grammatical relationships within these two sentences, our chief difficulty lies with the meaning of *katechon*. Obviously the readers knew what was meant by this term (2:5), but equally obvious is the fact that all subsequent interpretation moves in the realm of conjecture because this term has neither antecedent usage in Jewish apocalyptic literature nor is it found subsequently in the writings of early Christians.

The traditional interpretation already found in Tertullian sees in the *katechon* the restraining and ordering power of the Roman empire and of the Roman emperor respectively. This interpretation is certainly wrong because in the NT the Roman emperor or the empire do not have an eschatological significance. Moreover, apocalyptic texts in general do not look favorably upon the established secular powers, but regard them as perpetrators of evil, not as restrainers of evil. Furthermore, there would be no need to use such a strange veiled word like *katechon* if the author in fact assigns a praiseworthy function to the empire as the restrainer of the ultimate evil. Finally, we might remember that our readers were experiencing persecution.

Cullmann's interpretation sees in the *katechon* the gospel and the apostle—Paul himself. Yet if Paul actually had told the Thessalonians that the Rebel will appear only after he, Paul, is "out of the way" (2:7) then it is ununderstandable how the Thessalonians could have gotten the idea that "the Day of the Lord is present" when Paul himself was still alive. Also Munk's interpretation ignores the fact that, according to 1 Thess. 4:13–18, Paul expected to be alive at the parousia, nor could the Thessalonians have gotten the idea that a few months after Paul had left them he had preached the gospel representatively to the gentiles.

Another approach argues that the *katechon* is none other than God himself, who "delays" the End, or who "restrains" the mystery of rebellion. When God "withdraws" then the Rebel will be revealed. The difficulty with this interpretation is that there is no reason why our writer should not have written the word "God" or "God's plan" instead of using the strange word *katechon*. Nor would the reader understand that *ek mesou genētai* means "to withdraw." Its normal meaning is "to be out of the way."

We skip over the identification of the *katechon* as a mythical being, like the archangel Michael restraining the devil (Dibelius, pp. 47–51) and turn to an interpretation which opens a new understanding of this verse. The verb *katechein* can have either positive or negative connotations according to its context. While Schaefer argued in 1890 that the *katechōn* is none other than *Satan,* Giblin in his recent monograph interpreted the *katechon* as seizing, ecstatic, frenzied, prophetic power and the *katechōn* as one particular Christian prophet who in ecstasy proclaimed the presence of the Lord's day. His ouster from the Thessalonian church is the condition for the revelation of the Rebel. But we may ask why an individual ecstatic prophet in a local church and his expulsion should have such an eschatological, universal significance? This is not made clear by Giblin.

Perhaps we should, with Augustine, acknowledge that we do not know what and whom our writer meant by *katechon*. The relativity and hypothetical character of the following attempt at interpretation is therefore freely acknowledged. While vv. 3–4 and 8–9 refer to the *future* and contain traditional material, we note that v. 5 speaks of the apostle's *past* teaching and vv. 6–7 of the *present* knowledge of the readers and of the present activity of the *katechon*. We conclude that vv. 5–7 are the author's own additions and comments on an apocalyptic tradition. Next we note the breadth of meaning which the verb *katechein* has, used here as participle with the force of a quasi-title. It can mean "to grab," "seize," "restrain," "oppress," "detain," "possess," "occupy," etc. Finally, we recall that in his thanksgiving our author highlighted the persecution endured by his readers in the *present* and in 2:6 he speaks of their *present* knowledge and experience of the *katechon*. Therefore we shall translate *katechon* as "oppression" and "Oppressor." It should also be pointed out that the Greek text in distinction to the RSV has no explicit, direct object connected with *katechon* in vv. 5 and 7.

This leaves us with the difficult question of why our author speaks of *katechon* instead of persecution and tribulation (1:4). We suggest that our author made use of this word because pagans justified their anti-Christian activity with precisely this same word. To them it meant "restraining" the abominable Christian superstition. The oppressor-restrainer of v. 7 appears to be an ad hoc formulation by our author on the basis of the *katechon*, oppression, of v. 5 and refers to the leader who is behind the persecution of the Christians. He might have been a magistrate, the governor of a province, or even the emperor himself. While his identity is unknown to us it was not unknown to the readers.

V. 6 states that the present oppression lasts until the revelation of the Rebel and thus *distinguishes* the present from the future. In v. 7 our author shows the hidden *connection* between the present and the future "for the mystery of rebellion is already at work." Even as the future Rebel will be Satan's supreme agent, so Satan is active in the present. The effect of his present activity is "the mystery of rebellion" which calls the reader to decide for or against God and the gospel in the present. This present force of rebellion will later come to a climax in the Rebel and the Rebel will make his appearance when the preceding figure of the Oppressor has left the scene of history. We are reminded of the succession of evil powers pictured as beasts in the Book of Revelation which climaxed in a supreme satanic figure. In our text there are only two such figures—the Rebel and his predecessor, the Oppressor, who fancies himself to be a restrainer. In short, the *katechon* represents the present power of rebellion in the world. The readers are told that in the Oppressor's oppression the mystery of rebellion is already at work. Their oppression is the work of "those who do not know God" and who "do not obey the gospel of our Lord Jesus" (1:8b), that is, those who rebel in the present. But the climax of evil is yet to come in the appearance of the great deceiver (2:8-10). The last word, however, does not belong to the Rebel and the ultimate stage is not the apostasy effected by him, but the final act is Christ's destruction of the Rebel (2:8b) and of those who "refused to love the truth" (2:10b), but instead "believe the lie" (2:11), be it in the present or in the future.

The section 2:1-12 begins by warning against apocalyptic enthusiasm and ends with the assurance of the sovereignty of Christ who himself wages the holy war against the Rebel. Without the cooperation of his people, he will destroy the enemy and those who belong to him. While "the Day of the Lord" could not have been present already, it will surely come and mark Christ's victory over Satan's agent. The experience of the present oppression is not the experience of the messianic woes, but rather the experience of the present form of rebellion caused by the Oppressor who shall give way to the Rebel yet to come. Thus our writer claimed that history prior to the Day of the Lord has two periods—the period of oppression in which his readers find themselves and the period of the apostasy. Both periods are represented by a nameless figure, the Oppressor and the Rebel.

Our section also admonishes the readers to "remember" Paul's teaching (2:5). This theme is repeated in 2:15; 3:6; and 3:14. The tradition originating from Paul consists not only of an apocalyptic timetable, but also of ethical commandments. Eschatology is not theologically connected with ethics in this letter but both exist side by side. Ethical exhortation has become the issuing of commandments and ordinances (3:4, 6, 10, 12). Important is the motif of the necessity (*dei*) of imitating Paul (3:7, 9) who embodies the tradition. The first explicit imperative in our letter reads: "So then, brothers, stand firm and hold to the traditions (plural) which you were taught by us either by word of mouth or by letter." The source of the tradition is twofold, the oral apostolic word and the Pauline letter.

This imperative finds new expression in the prayer that our Lord "may comfort your hearts and establish them in every good work and word" (2:17). That which is commanded of Christians is simultaneously the content of prayer, which means that in our letter ethics is related to worship rather than to eschatology.

The apocalyptic emphasis in our author's Christology and the absence of the kerygma of the cross and resurrection did not lead him to expound the idea of an absent Christ. On the contrary, because the Lord is "with" the believers (3:16) and because "grace" and "peace" come from him, therefore prayers are addressed to him and commands and ordinances are issued in his name (3:6). Because the Lord is "faithful" (3:3) and present with his church, therefore he directs the hearts of his faithful people "to the love toward God and to the patient expectation of Christ" (3:5) who at his parousia will give "peace" (1:7) and "glory" (2:14) to those whom God has chosen from the beginning (2:13) and whom he called to faith through the gospel (2:14). Where the gospel is not obeyed (1:8), there God himself deludes the minds of unbelievers, "so that they may be condemned" (2:11 f.). Unbelief appears here as both a conscious decision against the gospel and as the result of God's action, and one cannot be played off against the other.

The problem of evil within the community receives an evangelical answer: "Keep away" from him (3:6); do not associate with him (3:14), lest he thinks that his lifestyle is acceptable in the church. There must be a clear "No" to evil within the community. Simultaneously, "do not look on him as an enemy, but warn him as a brother" (3:15). The purpose of church discipline must be to win the erring brother.

In conclusion, the purpose of 2 Thessalonians was 1) to counteract a specific form of apocalyptic enthusiasm; 2) to admonish the idle to stop living off the community and go to work; 3) to admonish all to hold on to Pauline traditions; 4) to warn against a pseudonymous Pauline letter. Above all, our letter endeavors to preserve the Pauline heritage against other forms of Pauline Christianity. In this struggle our author made use of non-Pauline traditions which he interpreted and actualized; and he used the literary form of a pseudonymous letter.

Indeed, he was a true upholder of Paul's heritage because he understood that what was decisive was not the imminence of the parousia, but the assurance of Christ's ultimate victory in spite of present afflictions, and simultaneously the commitment to a lifestyle of sobermindedness that is able to do the work at hand.

THE PASTORAL EPISTLES

THE NAME PASTORAL

The term "pastoral" as a designation of 1 and 2 Timothy and Titus is not ancient. It was first used by the Lutheran scholar, Paul Anton, of Halle, Germany, in 1726. He called them "pastoral" epistles because they are written by a pastor for pastors. However, this is not an exhaustive definition of their content. They contain a good deal of useful material for congregations, and have always been read with profit by the laity as well as by the clergy. They deal not only with what pastors ought to do, but also with what the laity should do, both in worship (e.g., 1 Tim. 2:8) and in everyday life (e.g., 1 Tim. 4:4–5).

THE PROBLEM OF AUTHORSHIP

Traditionally, and even in the RSV, the three letters, 1 and 2 Timothy and Titus, have always been ascribed to Paul. But since the rise of biblical criticism, the Pauline authorship of the Pastorals has been widely questioned, not only by radicals such as the Tübingen school in the nineteenth century and the Bultmann school in the twentieth, but also by comparatively conservative critics in Britain and America, as well as in Germany. There are four main reasons for this questioning of their Pauline authorship. First, the earliest codex of Pauline writings stops at 1 Thess. 5:5 (Chester Beatty Papyrus #46). But since this papyrus breaks off before the end of a book, it is possible that the original copy included the Pastorals. So we cannot be sure: it is not a conclusive argument against Pauline authorship. A further argument of similar character is that Marcion (A.D. 160) did not include the Pastorals in his canon. Of course, he might have rejected them as he rejected much else which was available. But this is unlikely, for there is very little use of the OT in the Pastorals to which Marcion might have taken exception on theological grounds. The Muratorian canon (c. A.D. 180) does include the Pastorals, but only as an appendix to the Pauline corpus. This suggests that toward the end of the second century they were only just beginning to make their way into the Pauline corpus.

A second argument against the authenticity of the Pastorals is their religious and theological character. In a rather unguarded moment, the late Professor Burton Scott Easton observed: "Paul was inspired, the Pastorals are orthodox." The contrast between inspiration and orthodoxy is a little unfortunate, but let that pass. The point is well taken. Paul is a much more adventurous and creative thinker, willing to take risks; the Pastor (as Easton conveniently calls the author of the Pastorals) is much more conventional and humdrum. He considers faith not so much in terms of personal commitment, but as a body of propositions to be believed (see e.g., 1 Tim. 1:19). He lays a remarkable stress on good works (see e.g., 1 Tim. 2:10; 5:10; 6:8; 2 Tim. 2:21; Tit. 2:14). Of course, Paul himself is just as concerned about the place of good works in the Christian life, but he more characteristically speaks of them as, e.g., the fruit of the Spirit. There is a difference of nuance in their presentation of the message of justification. It is not so much, as Easton rashly stated, that the Pastor attributed justification to the sacraments rather than to faith (on the basis of Tit. 3:5). Both authors agree that on God's side justification is the gift of God's grace (Tit. 3:7), and Paul would have agreed that the sacraments are means of grace. But on the human side there is a difference; Paul spoke of justification through faith (alone); the Pastor tends to think of justification as the outcome on the human side of both faith and works.

There are different nuances in the Pastor's Christology. While Paul can very occasionally speak of Christ as Savior (cf. Phil. 3:30—in an eschatological context), the Pastor regularly uses "Savior" as a title for Christ as well as for God in a way that suggests a stronger dose of Hellenistic religiosity (in Hellenistic milieu the title Savior, *Sōtēr*, could be used both of mystery and other cult deities and also for the Roman emperor). Thus, *Sōtēr*

is used for God at 1 Tim. 1:1; 2:3; 4:10; Tit. 1:3; 2:10; 3:4 and
for Christ at 2 Tim. 1:10; Tit. 1:4; 2:13; 3:6. Another favorite
term with similar cultic associations is "epiphany," which can be
used both of the first and of the second comings. Thus the Pastor
can speak of the "epiphany," of our Savior Christ Jesus, who
"abolished death and brought life and immortality to light" (2
Tim. 1:9 f.). Or again, he can speak of the future "hope of the
epiphany of our great God and Savior Jesus Christ" (Tit. 2:13).
As Rawlinson remarked, it is difficult to think of such expressions
being written by Paul.

On the negative side, we note the absence of a number of key
Pauline concepts. We hear nothing of the phrase "in Christ"
and the indwelling Spirit figures in only two places (2 Tim. 1:14;
Tit. 3:5). It is hard to avoid the conclusion that a different religious mind is at work in the Pastorals. And it is a second
generation mind.

There are marked differences of vocabulary between the Paulines and the Pastorals. The Pastoral Epistles contain an estimated
360 words not to be found in the genuine letters. Some of these
new words are especially frequent and convey a very different
impression, such as *eusebeia* (piety or religion), sound doctrine,
sobriety—the sort of vocabulary which reminds us of eighteenth
century tombstones. This new vocabulary is closely related to
Jewish-Hellenistic popular philosophy and ethics. The church
is settling down in the world and is appropriating conventional
categories of religion and ethics.

Although it is difficult to assess such matters objectively, there
is a real difference of style in the writing of the Pastorals. Easton
has contrasted what he calls the "prim preciseness" of the Pastor
with the "flood of eloquence" shown by Paul. So much for the
arguments *against* Pauline authorship.

At the same time, notable scholars have put up strong arguments for the authenticity of the Pastorals. They include J.
Jeremias and J. N. D. Kelly. Here are some of Jeremias'
arguments:

First, the addresses and conclusions of Paul's letters are characteristic and exhibit a development which starts with 1 Thessalonians

and ends with the Pastorals. The Pastorals in this respect start at
the point reached by Colossians and develop the addresses and
conclusions further from there. From Galatians onward Paul
speaks of himself as an apostle. From Romans on Paul alone is
the sender. 2 Thessalonians marks the beginning of a longer form
of the introductory greeting, while conversely the closing greeting, "Grace be unto you" gets shorter from Colossians on. Jeremias agrees with the German scholar, O. Roller, that it is impro-
able that such minutiae as these should have been the result of
forgery.

Second, unlike Easton, Jeremias stresses the theological affinities
between Paul and the Pastorals. For instance, Jesus Christ is the
revelation of God's mercy (1 Tim. 1:12, 17). Jesus Christ is the
new Man (1 Tim. 2:5). Justification is by grace (Tit. 3:7—
Jeremias is right here against Easton); it is through faith alone, not
by works (2 Tim. 1:9; 3:15; Tit. 3:5). The vicarious nature of
Christ's suffering is emphasized at 2 Tim. 2:10. Jeremias' doctrinal arguments contain a salutary warning against exaggerating
the differences between Paul and the Pastorals in doctrine, but they
are not conclusive arguments for the authenticity of the Pastorals.

Third, there is the personal testimony of Paul. Jeremias cites 1
Tim. 1:12–16, 2 Tim. 3:10–12 and 4:4–8. Here "Paul" speaks
of his readiness to suffer, of the strength of his faith. But the first
of these three passages appears to support the contrary argument:
this is just the sort of thing a deutero-Pauline writer would have
introduced for the sake of verisimilitude. The two passages from
2 Timothy are probably fragments of Paul's farewell letter to
Timothy (see below) and therefore do not affect our assessment of
the Pastorals as a whole.

Fourth, Jeremias argues that the positive or high doctrine of the
state of the Pastorals (1 Tim. 2:1 ff.; Tit. 3:1) is very similar to
that of the undoubted letters (Romans 13), and stands in sharp
contrast e.g., to that of Revelation. There is no reference to the
prospect of general martyrdom in the Pastorals, thus suggesting an
earlier date. But such teaching on the state was a commonplace
of primitive Christian catechesis and does not argue for the same
author. Similar teaching is found in 1 Pet. 3:13–17.

Fifth, Gnosticism is allegedly in the same state of development
as in Colossians; it is still a movement within the church. Against
this we may note that even in 1 John, written at the end of the first
century, the Gnostics troubling that community had only recently
seceded. Their secession could hardly have happened everywhere
at once, and this is no help for dating our documents.

Sixth, the ministry of presbyter-bishops found in the Pastorals, according to Jeremias, is in exactly the same state of development as in Philippians (1:1—bishops and deacons), and less advanced than at the turn of the first–second centuries. There is as yet no sign of "monepiscopacy" as in the epistles of Ignatius, and ordination is performed by the presbyterate (1 Tim. 4:14). This is a highly technical question, and our assessment of this argument must await fuller discussion later.

Seventh, the portrait of Timothy is not flattering. There are hints about his lack of stamina (2 Tim. 2:3, 12, 22). He is youthful and inexperienced, and perhaps not to be trusted with women (1 Tim. 5:2). Far from arguing for the genuineness of the Pastorals, these features actually militate against it. For in the genuine Pauline letters Timothy is a mature and responsible colleague of the apostle, the joint author of 1 and 2 Thessalonians, of 2 Corinthians, Philippians, Colossians, and Philemon. He is entrusted with responsible tasks (1 Cor. 4:17). In Phil. 2:19 Paul says he has no one like him. Admittedly, Timothy was not too successful with the Corinthians, but Paul never blamed him for that.

While recognizing the differences between the earlier Paulines and Pastorals, Jermias prefers to explain these by the so-called secretary hypothesis. Paul would not dictate letters in prison, but would write out the themes he wanted covered on wax tablets. The amanuensis would then take away the notes, write out the letters in full, and return them to Paul for approval and signature. But would an amanuensis draw on codes, quotations of hymns, etc. and to such an extent as happens in the Pastorals?

In Britain, a middle solution has been much favored, that of P. N. Harrison. He recognized several genuine Pauline fragments, and sought to fit them into Paul's life as covered by Acts.

A more radical position was offered by B. S. Easton. He was very guarded about the possibility of genuine fragments. He proposed that the Pastorals were written in the order: 2 Timothy, Titus, 1 Timothy. He offered several reasons for this. First, this sequence corresponds to the development of church order in the letters. In 2 Timothy the recipient is ordered to appoint "faithful men" as tradition-bearers. In Titus elders (note the formal designation, suggesting for the first time a fixed office) are to be installed in every city. In 1 Timothy the existence of elders is taken for granted, and rules are now laid down for their recruit-

ment, remuneration, and discipline. In 2 Timothy ordination is
by the apostle alone. In 1 Timothy it is by elders. Easton calls
this "a catholic revival of Jewish precedent."

Second, the position with regard to heresy changes. In 2 Tim.
2:17, 20 the heretics, Hymenaeus and Philetus, are still within the
church. In Tit. 3:10 heretics when obdurate are to be excom-
municated. In 1 Tim. 1:20 Hymenaeus has been delivered to
Satan.

Third, there is a decrease in personal, Pauline notes. There is
considerable material of this kind in 2 Timothy (especially
4:9–22). In Titus there is much less, only 3:12–15. But such
matter is completely lacking in 1 Timothy. This means that the
writer by now was able to stand on his own feet!

How then does Easton date the letter? 2 Timothy was written
when Gnosticism was becoming an acute danger, though still a
movement within the church. A wholly Christian generation was
growing up: the churches were no longer exclusively made up of
converts. The use of Acts (which Easton dates A.D. 90–93) is
suggested by the reference to Antioch, Iconium, and Lystra in
2 Timothy 3:11. Therefore Easton dates 2 Timothy *circa* A.D.
95, Titus A.D. 100 and 1 Timothy A.D. 105, i.e., a few years before Ignatius' letters. We find in 1 Timothy monarchical episco-
pacy in all but name, the term episcopus and presbyter still being
more or less synonymous.

What position are we to adopt among these three alternatives?
Jeremias, as we have shown, has not proved his case. Harrison's
piecing together of fragments is very complicated and implies an
artificial scissors-and-paste technique. I suggest that Easton was
right about the sequence. 2 Timothy is the earliest. This letter
is based upon one probably genuine Pauline fragment, the farewell letter of Paul to Timothy written in Rome during his imprisonment there shortly before his martyrdom (at the end of the
two years mentioned at the close of Acts?). The Pastor takes
this letter as his basis and expands it. He represents Paul as
setting out a church order, ethical teaching, and injunctions for
the battles against Gnosticism. 2 Timothy, thus expanded, serves
very much the same function as Paul's farewell address to the

elders of Ephesus in Acts 20, a Lukan composition, and there may well have been a close connection between the two authors (C. F. D. Moule even suggested that Acts and the Pastorals might be by the same author). The Pastor's initial efforts were further developed in Titus and finally in 1 Timothy.

What date is likely? Easton's dating of Acts is a little on the late side, and, in any case, 2 Tim. 3:10, 11, on which he bases his case, occurs in one of Harrison's genuine fragments (and, as I believe, is from Paul's genuine farewell letter). Also, Easton dates the Pastorals too close to Ignatius to allow time for development of monepiscopacy in so many churches in Asia Minor (and not just at Antioch, where it probably first developed). While unable to give a precise date, I would suggest that the Pastorals were the product of the generation after Paul's death; in other words, they were written somewhere between *circa* A.D. 65 to 90. The purpose of their composition was to grapple with the problem occasioned by the death of the apostles and the growth of false teachings.

THE COMPOSITION OF THE PASTORALS

Taking the Pastorals in Easton's order, we begin with 2 Timothy. The purported situation is one of imprisonment (1:8). This is not just the house arrest of Acts 28:30–31, but a more severe incarceration, for the apostle is in fetters (2:9). Either we must suppose (or the Pastor presupposes) that the two year period covered by the end of Acts has now come to an end with Paul's strict imprisonment, or else we must suppose (or the Pastor presupposes) that Paul was freed at the end of the two years, and went on further missionary journeys (either Spain, as a tradition beginning with 1 Clement has it, or in the East, as the Epistle to Titus suggests—though this seems to be contradicted by Acts 20:25, 38). At the end of this supposed journey, the apostle will have returned to Rome, been arrested, and committed to close confinement. He has, according to 2 Tim. 4:16 f., already faced a first hearing, which has gone well, but he expects a turn for the worse (4:6 ff.).

By subtracting those elements in 2 Timothy which refer to the heresy and the defensive measures against it, we are left with a considerable block of personal material. Either this material has been composed by the Pastor himself (on the basis of the genuine letters and Acts?) as a groundwork for his treatment of and response to the false teaching, or else he has lifted the personal material from a genuine farewell letter of Paul to Timothy. Such a letter could have included the following materials:

Chapter 1. Vv. 3–6, 8, 12, 15–18.
Chapter 2. Vv. 3–13.
Chapter 3. Vv. 10–11.
Chapter 4. Vv. 1–2, 6–22.

Into this personal letter (whether of his own construction, or from the genuine farewell letter), the Pastor will have inserted sections dealing with:

1. The preservations of apostolic tradition. The means for this (a succession of faithful men) are stated in 2:1–2. The content of the tradition is suggested in the hymn of 1:9–11.
2. A condemnation of the false teaching (2:14 through chap. 3, but excluding the personal material in vv. 10–11; chap. 4, vv. 2?, 3–4, 5?)

2 Timothy was the Pastor's first attempt to combat the heresy. In Titus he follows this first essay with a more systematized church order. Did he again have another genuine Pauline fragment on which to base his second effort? Harrison thought so, and identified it with 3:12–15. But the evidence is not so strong, and perhaps, having no more genuine materials, he constructed the personal references out of Acts (though Artemas and Zenas are not mentioned in Acts). Here is the structure of Titus:

1:1–4. Greeting.
1:5–9. Church order: qualifications for office bearers.
1:10–16. Attack on the heresy.
2:1–3:7. Christian ethics (in view of the heresy).
3:8–11. Return to the attack on the heresy.
3:12–15. Epistulary conclusion.

1 Timothy will be the latest of the three letters. It contains no personal notes. The author is now able to stand on his own feet, unless perchance he had no more genuine materials to utilize.

1:3 contains a vague personal note to give verisimilitude, but it presupposes no real, concrete situation, as did the personal notes of 2 Timothy and to a lesser degree in the letter to Titus. This epistle contains the most fully developed attack on the heresy and the most developed church order. Here now is the structure of 1 Timothy:

> 1:1–2. Greeting.
> 1:3–20. Against the heretics (their false theology).
> 2:1–3:16. Church order.
> 4:1–11. Against the heretics (their false ethics).
> 4:12–6:19. Church order (the duties of "Timothy").
> 6:20–21. Epistulary conclusion.

THE HERESY OF THE PASTORALS
PASSAGES: 2 TIM. 2:16–3:17; TIT. 1:10–16; 1 TIM. 1:3–20; 4:1–11.

Character. The heresy dealt with in the Pastorals exhibits a combination of speculative mythology with a rigid legalism and asceticism. The nature of the myths and genealogies referred to to is disputed. It was either a type a Hellenistic-Gnostic mythology, or it contained rabbinic fables and legends about the genealogies of the OT. Both interpretations are possible, because the heresy has points of contact both with Gnosis and with Judaism. On the Gnostic side we note that they held that the resurrection had already happened (2 Tim. 2:18). This will mean that like the Corinthian Gnosticizers, who denied the resurrection *from the dead,* (1 Corinthians 15) they will have believed that with their initiation they had already passed over into authentic existence and required no further eschatology. They denied the "not yet." Again, they claimed to "know" God—i.e., to have had an experience of Gnosis (Tit. 1:16; 1 Tim. 4:30 [see below]; 6:20). They held a dualistic world view which led them to eschew matrimony and to avoid certain kinds of food (1 Tim. 4:30; this verse also asserts the orthodox counter claim that *they,* not the Gnostics, are the ones who really "know" the truth). The reference to myths and to genealogies (1 Tim. 1:4; cf. 4:7; Tit. 3:9; 2 Tim. 4:4) could suggest the mythological hierarchies of the late second century Hellenistic Gnostic systems such as those of Valentinus and Basilides, though the reference in Tit. 1:14 to Jewish myths makes this problematical (see below).

On the other hand, there are distinctively Jewish features to the heresy. The myths in question are referred to in Tit. 1:14 as "Judaic" in character, and this reference has often been combined with the reference to "genealogies" in 1 Tim. 1:4 and that in Tit. 3:9, where genealogies appear in proximity to the law, to support the view that the allusion is to rabbinic speculations about OT genealogies. Definitely Jewish in character is the description of the heretics, or some of them, as belonging to the "circumcision party" (Tit. 1:10). And it is further stated in Tit. 3:9 (see above) that the heretics were involved in quarrels over the "law." Perhaps the way to reconcile these apparently contradictory pieces of evidence, some suggesting Hellenistic Gnosticism, others Jewish heresy, is to conclude that we have here an early form of Gnosticism which is largely, though eclectically Jewish in character. It is becoming more and more likely since the discovery of the Dead Sea Scrolls that Christian Gnosticism developed out of heterodox Judaism, and was not, as used to be supposed, Hellenistic in origin.

We have already noted that the heretics held a dualistic worldview, something which is quite un-Jewish. They were moving toward the position which comes out in the second century Gnostic systems, that the world was created by an inferior deity, for although such a view is not expressly attributed to them, they seem to have held the position that creation was evil (1 Tim. 4:1–5). This is why the Pastor is at pains to insist that creation is positively good (v. 4), and to insist that nothing in the created order is to be rejected so long as it is accepted as gift from the Creator. So much for their theology. On their Christology, the Pastor is even less explicit; but his emphasis on the incarnation perhaps suggests that the heretics were inclined to docetic views of Christology. For instance, he stresses in 2 Tim. 2:8 that Christ comes from the seed of David, and he cites the early Christian hymn (see below) to the effect that the Redeemer was manifested in the flesh (1 Tim. 3:16). But this insistence on the flesh of

Jesus is not so strong as it is in the polemics of 1 John, and we should be cautious in trying to infer too much from it.

Like much other anti-Gnostic literature of the period, the Pastorals indulge in a good deal of mud-slinging against their opponents. They are accused of being out for filthy lucre (Tit. 1:11; cf. 2 Tim. 3:6). They are accused of "beastliness" (Tit. 1:12). They are liars, lazy, and gluttonous (*ibid.*). This is a savage indictment, but it appears to be substantiated from other denunciations of the Gnostics through the second century, in Irenaeus and other Christian writers, and even from such fragments of Gnostic literature that have survived, including some of the recently discovered Nag Hammadi literature.

The Tübingen school (Mack, 1836) identified the heretics of the Pastorals with Marcion and his school. The clincher for this identification was found in the references to "antitheses," (1 Tim. 6:20), a word which Marcion used as a title for one of his works. But Marcion's teaching was generally different from that of the Pastorals, its chief feature being its opposition to the OT and Judaism. Also, the date of Marcion (*c*. A.D. 140) would make it necessary to place the Pastorals well after Ignatius (A.D. 110–115), whereas the church order of the Pastorals (see above) is more primitive than that of Ignatius.

CHURCH ORDER AND MINISTRY
IN THE PASTORALS

In 2 Timothy we hear of Timothy's ordination through the laying on of hands by the apostle (2 Tim. 1:6). This rite conveys the charisma of ministry. We may compare Acts 14:23 and 20:17 with this passage. Paul and Barnabas are stated to have ordained elders in every city on the first missionary journey, and Paul later addresses the elders of Ephesus.

In 2 Tim. 2:1–2, Timothy hands on the apostolic tradition to "faithful men," who are to hand it on to "others." This presupposes at least three generations of ministers, "Paul," "Timothy," "faithful men" and possibly four generations (if the "others" are the bearers of the tradition in the next generation, rather than the congregation to which the faithful men will minister). This responsibility for the tradition is similarly implied in the speech of Paul to the elders of Ephesus in Acts 20 (vv. 29 and 32).

Timothy is described in 2 Tim. 2:15 as one who handles the word of truth. It is his function rightly to "divide" (cut up) or expound this word, not just to preserve it. In 2:25 he is responsible for church discipline, for he is to "correct opponents."

In Tit. 1:5 Titus is to appoint (*katastēsēs*) elders in the cities of Crete according to the apostle's explicit instructions. But then from v. 7 onwards the Pastor speaks of the qualifications not of elders (*presbyteri*) in the plural, but of the *episcopus* in the singular. Some (e.g., such different writers as Austin Farrar and Günther Bornkamm) have held that the *episcopus* is a different functionary from the elders, and that we have here evidence for the development of monepiscopacy. Others explain the switch of titles and the switch from the plural to the singular as due to the combination of different sources. Most interpreters, however, explain the shift, take the elders and the bishops to refer to the same officers, and postulate a set-up for the Pastorals similar to that in Acts (cf., Acts 20:28, where *episcopus* = guardian, with 20:17), i.e., of presbyter-bishops, prior to the evolution of monepiscopacy. The function of these personages is not only to rule, but to exhort (*parakalein*). It is a preaching office. They must also oppose the heretics (*tous antilegontas elenchein*).

In 1:18 "Timothy" is said to have been ordained *kata tas proagousas epi se prophēteias*. This seems to mean that prophets formed a selection committee (cf. Acts 13:1–3). In 3:1–7 the qualifications of an *episcopus* (note again the singular as in Titus) and his functions are defined as "care" of the church of God (v. 5). In other words his primary task is that of ruler or administrator. But once more teaching (*didaskein*) is also mentioned.

In 3:8–12 we have the first occurrence in the Pastorals of deacons (*diakonoi*) with a statement of their qualifications. The Pastor stresses the requirement of financial integrity, which suggests that their function was the administration of charity. That seems to be the way the author of Acts views the seven in Acts 6, though he does not actually designate them by the noun "deacons" but only their function by the verb *diakonein*.

4:13 mentions the duties of Timothy in the congregation: reading, exhortation, and teaching (*anagnōsis, paraklēsis, didaskalia*). "Reading" means the public reading of the OT.

4:14 speaks of Timothy's ordination. This time it was performed by the laying on of hands *by the presbytery*: compare and contrast with this the language of 2 Tim. 1:6. The presbytery evidently form a collegium, and one might suppose that the apostle acted with the presbyters around him, very much as a modern bishop does. But the prophets still serve as a selection committee as in 2 Timothy.

It is very much disputed whether the sudden laying on of hands warned against in 5:22 is a reference to ordination, or whether, as the language about partaking in other men's sins may suggest, it is a reference to penitential practice, i.e., restoring of penitents to church fellowship. Jeremias, Lohse, Michaelis, and Schlier all take it to refer to ordination, while Galtier, Lock, Easton, and Dibelius interpret it to refer to penitential practice.

5:17 speaks of the honor and payment due to elders. The verse hints that while all elders ruled, some did better than others. And among them were also some who did not just rule but also labored in word and teaching. This suggests that we are still in a state of development from a patriarchal form of government to an ordained ministry.

5:19 speaks of disciplinary procedures to be used against refractory elders.

How are we to interpret this evidence? Apart from the widows (of whom more will be said later) it appears that the Pastorals envisage a sub-apostolic situation in which there are three types or grades of ministry. First, there is the position and the function occupied and performed by Timothy and Titus. This position is not given any particular name. But they carry out in a limited sphere the oversight of a plurality of congregations as the apostle had done in his lifetime.

Next, on the more likely interpretation, there are from Titus onwards presbyter-bishops. These appear as a committee to be responsible both for ruling the local congregation and to maintain doctrinal tradition, to preach the word and to refute heretics.

Then by the time of 1 Timothy we have a third grade, the deacons (*diakonoi*), whose qualifications suggest that their primary role was to administer relief of the poor.

The word *episcopus* occurs five times in the NT (Acts 20:28, Phil. 1:1; 1 Tim. 3:2; Tit. 1:7; and as a christological title, though suggesting a ministerial usage as its origin, in 1 Pet. 2:25).

What is the source of the title? Two suggestions have been made. First, that it comes from Hellenistic usage: the *episcopus* was a functionary in the Greek city state, a financial and legal officer. This suggestion was put forward by Edwin Hatch in the Bampton Lectures of 1880, and has been widely accepted. In favor of this theory it might be argued that the term *episcopus* does not appear in Christianity until the Hellenistic stage.

More recently it has been suggested that the term is of Jewish origin, coming from the Qumran usage. (Jeremias, R. E. Brown). In the description of the community's organization, the term *mᵉbaqqēr,* visitor or overseer, is used. His responsibilities are analogous to that of the NT *episcopus.* He preaches, teaches, and is responsible for the admission of converts. It is interesting to note that when they first appear in Christian literature (Phil. 1:1) there is a plurality of them in a congregation, as at Qumran.

Jeremias thought that the *episcopi* were not identical with the *presbyteri,* but that the latter were the older men of the community who formed a kind of governing committee, whereas the *episcopi* were chosen from among the *presbyteroi* as a whole for specific ministerial functions. This suggestion, neat and attractive though it may seem, is difficult to substantiate from the evidence.

We are probably wrong if we take the bishops and deacons of Phil. 1:1 as a formally organized ministry. Probably the set-up in Philippi was not basically different from that in Corinth and in the other Pauline churches. If so, we should perhaps interpret the bishops and deacons there as unordained charismatic officers who had, like Stephanas and his family in 1 Cor. 16:15, "set themselves" to do a task in the church for which they had special gifts.

The fact that at Philippi it is these charismatic officers, rather than teachers and prophets, who are designated by specific titles may be due to the important role the church at Philippi played in the sphere of finance and relief work. This was the only church that Paul allowed to contribute to his own welfare and to send him care packages when he was in prison, probably at Ephesus. Hence the relief officers there acquired specific titles which they did not have elsewhere. At Corinth, for instance, the services they performed were apparently known simply as "governments" and "helps" (1 Cor. 12:28). At the same time the developments which occurred at Philippi were important, for they set a pattern which was later taken up and developed further in the Pauline churches for a more permanent type of organized ministry. That is what we see happening both in the Pastorals and in Acts. How this development actually took place we shall discover after we have considered the next title, the *presbyteroi*.

Elders (*z^{e}kanim*) were a regular feature of Jewish communities. There was a body of elders both in the sanhedrin at Jerusalem and in the local synagogues in the diaspora. It appears that at Jerusalem a similar organization was adopted for the Christian community there. The first *certain* reference to such a body is in Acts 21:18. The earlier references (11:30; 15:2, 4, 6) are probably anachronisms. If this is so, we may infer that James and the elders replaced Peter and the twelve when he (and they?) left Jerusalem for good after the apostolic conference (Galatians 2; Acts 15). Was it James who personally introduced the presbyteral system into the Jerusalem church? Since other evidence (e.g., Matthew) seems to indicate that actual ministerial work (i.e., the ministry of the word) was performed in the Palestinian churches by prophets and teachers (for which there is also evidence in the Hellenistic Jewish churches outside of Palestine, see Acts 13:1), we may infer that initially at any rate the elders were simply a governing committee. But later on, both in the Palestinian and in the Hellenistic churches where they were introduced, the elders acquired ministerial functions. Thus, for instance, we find in Jas. 5:14 that the elders have taken over the charismatic function of healing. This gives a clue to the general development of ministry in the sub-apostolic age. As the charismata died out, the churches turned more and more to the presbyters to perform activities which had previously been in the hands of the charismatics. Something of this development seems to be discernible in the Didache, which speaks of elders substituting for prophets as the reciters of the eucharistic prayer. The same thing has happened by the time of the Pastorals with various forms of the ministry of the word.

The earlier charismatic ministries were not ordained (1 Cor. 16:15). They arose spontaneously in the communities and were recognized and accepted through the Spirit. But this situation could not last. As Eduard Lohse has shown, with the adoption of the Jewish system of elders there came into the church the Jewish practice of ordination by laying on of hands. The Jewish origin of this practice is indicated in the earliest ordination liturgy we have (that of Hippolytus, c. A.D. 200), which draws an analogy between the Christian elders and the Jewish elders. Hippolytus refers (as the Jewish ordination liturgy did) to the appointment of elders by Moses.

In the Judaism of NT times the practice of ordination was as follows: First, there was a period of time spent in the study of the tradition (Torah), and rabbinic interpretation, later codified, beginning with the Mishnah and culminating with the Talmud. When the period of study was completed there took place the rite known as *semikah*: three ordained scribes laid hands on the ordained in the context of a prayer which alluded to Moses' ordination of Joshua and/or the 70 (72) elders (Num. 27:18–23; Deut. 34:9). It was believed that through this rite the spirit of Moses, which had descended on Joshua and the original elders, was now being passed on to the newly ordained.

Although we have no evidence for it, we may infer from Hippolytus that this type of rite first entered into the Christian church via Jewish Christianity, and that it passed from thence to the Hellenistic churches, including the Pauline ones. This then is what we find in the Pastorals. First, the candidates were selected by the prophets' pointing out in the Spirit those who had been chosen (Acts 13:1–3; 1 Tim. 1:18; 4:14), after devotional preparation through prayer and fasting on the part of all. Next, the candidates were handed a creedal confession (2 Tim. 2:2) to which they solemnly assented (1 Tim. 6:12). Käsemann thought that the commandment of v. 14 (*entolē*) was an ordination charge. Then intercessory prayer would be offered for the candidates, after which the central act, the laying on of hands, would take place (Acts 6:6; 13:3; 1 Tim. 4:14; 2 Tim. 1:6). This type of laying on of hands must be distinguished from other types employed for different purposes, such as the laying on of hands for healing (Mark 6:5 by Jesus; Mark 16:18 by the eleven; Jas. 5:14 by the elders); the laying on of hands in connection with baptism, underlining and in some cases mediating the initiatory gift of the Spirit (Acts 8:17; 19:6; Heb. 6:2); and the laying on of hands upon penitents which may be referred to in 1 Tim. 5:22 (see above).

Who laid on hands? In 2 Tim. 1:6 it is "Paul" (cf. Acts 14:23). It is difficult to say whether, historically, apostles actually did lay on hands in their lifetime and it seems that the practice of ordination came into the church in the sub-apostolic age. In that case the Acts passages are anachronisms reflecting the practice in Luke's church. In the Pastorals, however, the imposition of hands is clearly expected to be performed by the Timothy or Titus type figures. We shall have to ask later what the basis for this was in the understanding of office in the apostolic age itself. In 1 Tim. 4:14 it is the presbytery as a corporate body that lays on hands. How are we to explain the difference between these two practices? Perhaps the author of the Pastorals thinks that initially, when a community was being established, the apostles laid hands on the first ministers; thereafter it was the corporate presbytery that was responsible for perpetuating itself. Maybe historically the intermediate figures such as Timothy and Titus, or what they stand for in the Pastorals, established the local ministries.

Ordination was not intended merely as a symbolic act. As in

Judaism, it was understood as an effective rite, an action by which the Spirit (charisma) was conveyed by God for the performance of ministry. 2 Tim. 1:6 describes what ordination conveys and how it works. Using later church language we would be justified in calling ordination as it is described in the Pastorals as a sacramental rite, though in accordance with Reformation theology we would not speak of it as a "sacrament," a term of honor reserved for the two sacraments of the gospel, baptism and the Lord's Supper.

On the basis of this analysis we will now proceed to reconstruct the historical development of ministry in early Christianity. In the earliest period, Peter and the twelve provided the essential foundation for the proclamation and life of the Christian church. They had the unique and inalienable function of witnessing to the Christ event of which they had had first hand experience, and were directly appointed by the risen Lord in resurrection appearances. They had the function of general oversight over the communities. As the church expanded they were assisted by other functionaries, mainly charismatic. Of these, the prophets and teachers were the most important. But alongside of this there developed, first in Jerusalem, a body of elders whose function was to superintend the communities in the absence of the twelve or the apostles. Some think that in Luke's sources the seven were really elders.

In the sub-apostolic age, as the apostles died out, their unique and unalienable function was perpetuated through the apostolic tradition. This crystallized in two forms, the creedal formulae or deposit of which the Pastorals speak, and the apostolic writings, whether authentic as in the case of the Pauline epistles, or pseudonymous as in the case of the Pastorals. For a time the handing on of this tradition was superintended by intermediate figures such as the Timothy and Titus of the Pastorals. These functionaries have no recognized name. Charles Gore called them apostolic men. Others have called them apostolic delegates, but that is a bit too formal and anachronistic, and for contemporary Roman Catholics it has unfortunate associations. Like the apostles, they seem to be able to intervene directly and order the affairs of local congregations over the heads of their local leaders, and to control the local leaders too. During this period there arose a local ministry consisting of (ordained) bishop-presbyters and deacons.

The third period takes us beyond the NT. This is the second-century arrangement known to Ignatius. Here the intermediate figures have disappeared; in the local churches there is emerging out of the presbyteries a single leader for whom the term *episcopus* is being increasingly used as a distinctive designation. This has not happened everywhere in Ignatius' time, for the position of Polycarp at Smyrna is unclear, and it looks as if there is as yet no single *episcopus* at Rome (!). But it indicates the direction in which the church is moving by the second century.

A crucial question is that of the links between these three periods. Many (especially Anglicans) would like to draw a direct link between the apostles, the "apostolic men," and the Ignatian *monepiscopus*. Did the apostles themselves make provision for their successors (the apostolic men), and did the apostolic men make provision for one member of the presbytery to emerge as *monepiscopus* and head over the rest of the presbyters? That was the view of history which was beginning to emerge during the period of the Pastorals, for it seems to be presupposed by the very fact of their Pauline pseudonymity and the same claim is advanced by 1 Clement. But we cannot tell if this is the truth or an aetiological myth. We have to bear in mind the tendency of the church from the second century onwards to ascribe all its customs (including in one place the waving of a fan over the consecrated elements at the eucharist to protect them from flies!) as the result of direct apostolic enactment.

The further question whether the development in the Pastorals is a legitimate one will be dealt with later when we discuss emergent catholicism in the NT.

THE ETHICS OF THE PASTORALS

Like the Acts of the Apostles, the Pastorals were written at a time when the church was coming to realize that it was here to stay. The author of Acts expressed this consciousness by writing a history of the community: earlier than that no one had thought

that such a history of the community was worth writing since
the church was not expected to go on here for long anyhow.
Similarly, now that Christians knew that the church was here to
stay, a much more positive attitude had to be taken toward institutions of society. Paul had written to the Corinthians that if
they were married (which actually he preferred them to be)
then they must be as though they were not. This is the Pauline
ethic *hōs mē,* "if now." The Pastorals, like the deutero-Pauline
writings (Colossians and Ephesians), take a much more positive
line. Christians must live as citizens of this world. They must
live up to their responsibilities as citizens, as husbands, wives, etc.
in all their social relationships (1 Tim. 2:15; 5:4, 14). Dibelius
described the ethic of the Pastorals as bourgeois. Is this fair?
The alternative was the dualistic asceticism of the Gnostics. The
Pastorals adopted a pattern of ethical teaching which had been
taken over by Hellenistic Jews from Stoicism, including the household codes (1 Tim. 2:1–10; Tit. 2:1–10), and the catalogues of
vices (2 Tim. 3:2–5; Tit. 3:3). All this may look very humdrum.
But Jeremias' comment is worth reciting: "With words taken from
the moral ideals of Greek ethics the Christian life is described by
three adverbs. In relation to the self it is a life of discipline
(*sophronōs*), in relation to the neighbor a life of justice (*dikaiōs*),
in relation to God it is a life of piety. What Greek ethics proposed
for a man to fulfill in his own strength, and therefore demanded
in vain, is now realized where the educative grace of God is at
work. Here is the great gulf between Christian and non-Christian
ethics, Jewish or Greek. Here the motive of morality is the
demand of the law, of reason, or of the conscience, which place
a man before a 'thou shalt,' which he cannot fulfill. Christianity
knows a new motive for ethics, which conveys power for its ful-
fillment—the gratitude of the adopted child of God for the divine
forgiveness in which the educative grace of God works itself out
as the power unto salvation."

There is one aspect of the household codes which has little appeal in an age of liberation, and this is the emphasis on subordination (see especially Tit. 2:5; 3:1–8a). Is this to be taken as a

timeless principle, to be demanded of Christians in the twentieth century no less than of those who lived in the first and second centuries? Or is it time-conditioned? In favor of the latter, it may be argued that the procedure of the sub-apostolic writers was to take over the household codes from outside sources (Hellenistic, Jewish, and Stoic) and to seek to transform these codes by the two principles of "in the Lord" (i.e., relationships between people were to be worked out as part of their obedience to Christ as *Kyrios*) and in *agapē* (i.e., the structures of society were to be inwardly transformed by the spirit of Christian love). It is arguable therefore that the principle of subordination which the codes express is not in itself the essence of the Christian ethic, but a given structure of social life which the essence of the Christian ethic has to transform. There would therefore be no point in appealing to the subordinationist code today in order to repristinate the structures of a bygone society and age. Rather, the task of contemporary Christian ethic is the same as it was in the time of the Pastor: to transform the structures of twentieth century society *en Kyrio* and *en agapē*.

This brings us to the vexing question of the position of women in the church. Paul had proclaimed in principle the equality of men and women in one ecclesia (Gal. 3:28). In 1 Corinthians he had hedged a bit on this: while allowing women to prophesy in church he required them to be veiled for reasons that are not quite clear (1 Cor. 11:2–16) but certainly involved a recognition of woman's subordinate status. But the injunction that they should keep silence in the churches in 1 Cor. 14:34–36 is probably an interpolation from the same hand that wrote 1 Tim. 2:12–15. What happened to Paul's eschatological woman? The answer seems to be that by the time of the Pastorals she had become a Gnostic! The Pastor represents a conservative reaction to Gnostic abuses (cf. 2 Tim. 3:6–7; Rev. 2:20). After the first flush of enthusiasm, the church reverted to Jewish custom in this matter. Most recently these texts (1 Cor. 14:34–36 and 1 Tim. 2:12–15) have been used by conservative opponents of the ordination of women in the Anglican church in Australia. Is

this a legitimate interpretation? It would be, if there were a contemporary danger that women would prove heretical in the pulpit.
But since the dangers of heresy are no greater and no less with
women than they are with male preachers today, scriptural obedience no longer seems to require that women keep silent in the
churches. Still less can the principle of subordination be involved
as a theological grounding for the same end.

If the Pastor does not permit women to have any share in the
ministry of the word (he says nothing of the ministry of the
sacraments; we may assume that he knew of the eucharist, as he
certainly knew of baptism—but like most other NT writers is
quite uninterested in the question of who administers them) he
does allow certain other ministerial acts to be performed by them.
He has a formally constituted "order" of widows, whose qualifications suggest that they were permitted to perform services in the
name of the church, similar to those performed by the male
deacons (1 Tim. 5:3-8). There is other evidence in early Christianity for the existence of an order of widows (cf. *Didascalia* III
1-11). Interpreters are at variance as to whether the author
further recognizes an order of "deaconesses" distinct from that
of widows. There is an ambiguity at 1 Tim. 3:11; "the woman"
could mean either female deacons or the wives of deacons.

THE DEPOSIT

One of the key theological ideas of the Pastor is that of
"deposit." The term occurs three times (1 Tim. 6:20; 2 Tim.
1:12, 14). The deposit is handed over to Timothy at his ordination; it is his responsibility to preserve it intact and to hand it
over inviolate to faithful men, presumably at their ordination.
Unfortunately, the author does not spell out in detail what precisely the content of the deposit was. We may assume that it
consisted of the apostolic tradition expressed in creedal formulae
and hymns. Such formulae are cited at several places in the
Pastorals. They are christological in character. Sometimes they
are referred to as "faithful sayings," as, for instance, the well-
known saying, "Christ Jesus came into the world to save sinners"

(1 Tim. 1:15; cf. 3:1; 4:9; 2 Tim. 2:11; Tit. 1:9; 3:8). Some of them are apparently dominical sayings in a developed form:

> If we have died with him,
>   we shall also live with him;
> If we endure,
>   we shall also reign with him;
> If we deny him,
>   he also will deny us;
> If we are faithless,
>   he remains faithful—
> For he cannot deny himself
>
> (2 Tim. 2:11–13).

The original nucleus of this faithful saying seems to be discernible in the dominical logion Luke 12:8 f. par. (Q).

Another type of tradition which is cited in the Pastorals is hymnic. The best known example is the christological confession:

> (Who) was manifested in the flesh.
> vindicated in the Spirit
>   seen by angels,
> preached among the nations,
> believed on in the world
>   taken up in glory
>
> (1 Tim. 3:16).

It is clear from such identifiable items in the "deposit" that the Pastor was not a creative theologian. His reaction to the situation in his day is simply that of holding action: guard the deposit! Hold on to it through thick and thin. Preserve it inviolate. Hold it out against heretics as a refutation of their position. Tighten up the organization of the church so as to facilitate this holding action. The Pastor makes no attempt to come to grips theologically with the heretics by independent argumentation. In all of this he stands in sharp contrast to the writers of the Johannine school, or even to the deutero-Pauline author of Ephesians. At his worst he descends to name-calling as in the hexameter (quoted at

Tit. 1:12) "Cretans are always liars, evil beasts, lazy gluttons."
But this is only an occasional worst, not his sole weapon, as it
was for the author of the Letter of Jude.

EMERGING CATHOLICISM IN
THE NEW TESTAMENT

The Pastoral Epistles confront us more completely and sys-
tematically than any of the other NT writings with the phenomenon of *Frühkatholizismus* (early, or emerging catholicism in the
NT). With the delay in the parousia, the death of the original
witnesses to the Christ event (Peter and the twelve, James and
all the apostles: see 1 Cor. 15:5–7) and the increasing threat of
Gnosticism, the church responded by developing such institutional
features as the deposit, the regularly ordained ministry of
presbyter-bishops (to evolve after NT times into a monepiscopacy
presiding over a corporate presbytery with deacons) and a struc-
tured cathechism.

The recognition of these developments in the later writings of the
NT was an achievement of the Tübingen school (F. C. Baur and his
pupils) in the nineteenth century, although the late datings which
they proposed for these writings have since been significantly modified. The recognition of emerging catholicism in the NT has frequently been accompanied by a negative assessment of it. Ernst
Käsemann, for instance, looked back wistfully to the free charismatic
order of the Pauline churches, and thought that only this set-up was
compatible with the Pauline message of justification by grace through
faith apart from the works of the law.

Conservative reaction has been to argue for the Pauline authenticity of the Pastorals and then either to deny that the institutional
elements are in any sense "catholic" (so, e.g., the Barthian systema-
tician, H. Diem) or alternatively, frankly accepting them as catholic,
and so seeking Pauline sanction for catholicism (so, e.g., the high
church Anglican scholar, H. J. Carpenter). Either way, the process
of institutionalization was read back into the apostolic age and the
alleged incompatibility between the apostolic gospel and the institu-
tion thus overcome.

The Roman Catholic systematic theologian, Hans Küng, has
taken a different line. Accepting the critical conclusion that the
Pastorals are post-Pauline and positively welcoming the recognition of emerging catholicism in the NT, he found in the NT a tra-

jectory leading from the free-charismatic ministry of the Pauline churches through the incipient institutionalization of the ministry in the Pastorals to the post NT development first of monepiscopacy and finally of the Papacy.

What choice can we make between these various assessments of the Pastorals? Critical method, as we have shown, requires that we recognize the development from the free-charismatic to the regular institutionalized ministry, and the consequent presence of emerging catholicism within the NT. But is this necessarily a corruption of the Pauline gospel? We would argue not. The seeds of the later development are already present in Paul. For him, too, the gospel can be handed on as tradition (1 Cor. 15:1–3). And for him, too, the free–charismatic ministry was subject to apostolic control—hence the energy with which he wrote 1 Corinthians. For the Holy Spirit was present only where *Jesus* was confessed as Lord, that is, the Jesus who lived on earth and was crucified, i.e., the Jesus of the apostolic witness and of the church's confession. It was the function of the apostle to hold the charismata to that witness and to that confession. The element of apostolic control which is attested by the writing of 1 Corinthians has in some way to be perpetuated in the church. And the church in the sub-apostolic age, as evidenced by the Pastorals, evolved its institutions to perpetuate that control. A regularly ordained ministry, in which the deposit was entrusted at ordination by one generation of ministers to another in succession, was developed as a means of perpetuating the control of the charismata by the apostolic testimony. A third institutional element, the canon of NT scriptures, is not explicitly mentioned in the Pastorals (contrast 2 Pet. 3:15–16). But the Pastor seems to presume the existence of a Pauline corpus and probably also the Acts of the Apostles as well as Jesus tradition, all of which he brings to bear on the problem of keeping the church faithful to the apostolic gospel.

Of course, there were dangers in this situation. We have already pointed out the uncreative quality of the Pastor's response to the Gnostic heresy. But the preservation of the deposit—including, later, all the Pauline writings—created the possibility for a Johannine school, a Tertullian, an Augustine, a Luther, a Wesley, and a Karl Barth to unfreeze the deposit and make it come alive again as a kerygma. The Pastorals do not provide us with a blue-print of the church's institutions for all time. But they witness to the necessity of institutions. And by pointing back to the Pauline kerygma they also witness to the need for every generation to recover the *viva vox evangelii*. In this sense they merit their place in the canon.

SELECTED BIBLIOGRAPHIES

EPHESIANS

ABBOTT, T.K. *Epistles to the Ephesians and to the Colossians.*
ICC (Edinburgh: T. & T. Clark, 1897).

ROBINSON, J. A. *St. Paul's Epistle to the Ephesians.* (London:
Clark, no date).

WESTCOTT, B. F. *Saint Paul's Epistle to the Ephesians.* (London:
Macmillan, 1906).

SCOTT, E. F. *The Epistles of Paul to the Colossians, to Philemon
and to the Ephesians.* (New York: Harper, 1930).

GOODSPEED, E. J. *The Meaning of Ephesians.* (Chicago: University of Chicago Press, 1933).

BARTH, MARKUS. *Ephesians; Introduction. Translation and Commentary.* 2 vols. The Anchor Bible. (Garden City: Doubleday,
1974).

CAIRD, G. B. *Paul's Letters from Prison.* (London: Oxford University Press, 1976).

COLOSSIANS

BUJARD, WALTER. *Stilanalytische Untersuchungen zum Kolosserbrief als Beitrag zur Methodik von Sprachvergleichen.* Studien
zur Umwelt des Neuen Testaments 11. (Goettingen: Vandenhoeck & Ruprecht, 1973).

CROUCH, JAMES E. *The Origin and Intention of the Colossian
Haustafel.* FRLANT 109. (Goettingen: Vandenhoeck & Ruprecht, 1972).

LAEHNEMANN, JOHANNES. *Der Kolosserbrief. Komposition, Situation und Argumentation.* SNT 3. (Guetersloh: Guetersloh Ver-
lagshaus Gerd Mohn, 1971).

LOHSE, EDUARD. *Colossians and Philemon. A Commentary on the Epistles to the Colossians and to Philemon,* tr. W. R. Poehlmann and R. J. Karris. Hermenia. (Philadelphia: Fortress Press, 1971). The best commentary available in English.

SCHWEIZER, EDUARD. *Der Brief an die Kolosser.* EKK, NT. (Zuerich, Einsiedeln, Koeln: Benziger Verlag; und Neukirchen-Vluyn: Neukirchener Verlag, 1976). The best commentary available in German.

2 THESSALONIANS

FRAME, J. E. *A Critical and Exegetical Commentary on the Epistle of St. Paul to the Thessalonians.* ICC (New York: Scribner's, 1912). Still the best commentary in English.

BEST, E. *A Commentary on the First and Second Epistles to the Thessalonians.* BNTC. (London: Black, 1972). A mine of information with a balanced treatment of all difficulties.

MILLIGAN, G. *St. Paul's Epistles to the Thessalonians. The Greek Text with Introduction and Notes.* (London: Macmillan, 1908). An older but still very useful work.

RIGAUX, B. *Les épîtres aux Thessaloniciens.* Etudes bibliques. (Paris: Gembloux, 1956). The most detailed commentary.

TRILLING, W. *Untersuchungen zum 2. Thessalonicherbrief.* Erfurter Theologische Studien 27. (Leipzig, 1972).

GIBLIN, C. H. *The Threat to the Faith. An Exegetical and Theological Re-Examination of 2 Thes. 2.* Analecta Biblica 31. Rome, 1967.

JEWETT, R. "Enthusiastic Radicalism and the Thessalonian Correspondence," *Society of Biblical Literature 1972 Proceedings.* Vol. 1, 181–232.

AUS, R. D. article in *JBL* 92, 1973, 432–38.

BOERS, H. article in *NTS* 22, 1976, 140–58.

KAYE, B. N. article in *Nov. Test.* 17, 1975, 47–57.

THE PASTORALS

Some of the most important commentaries on the Pastorals are in German and have not been translated.

DIBELIUS, M. and CONZELMANN, H. *The Pastoral Epistles,* tr.

P. Buttolph and A. Yarbro. Hermenia. (Philadelphia: Fortress Press, 1972). The best commentary in English.

EASTON, B. S. *The Pastoral Epistles* (London: SCM, 1948).

KELLY, J. N. D. *A Commentary on the Pastoral Epistles* BNTC; (New York: Harper, 1963). A conservative commentary by an Anglican patristic scholar.

HANSON, A. T. *The Pastoral Letters* (Cambridge: U.P., 1966) An admirable, brief treatment, critically oriented.

Monographs:

CARPENTER, H. J. Art. "Minister, Ministry" in A. Richardson (ed.), *A Theological Word Book of the Bible* (London: SCM, 1950) 146–52.

HANSON, A. T. *Studies in the Pastoral Epistles* (London: SPCK, 1968). A series of essays on exegetical problems.

KAESEMANN, E. "Ministry and Community in the New Testament" in *Essays on New Testament Themes* (SBT 41; London: SCM 1964) 63–134.